HOTSPOTS
DOMIN
REPUBLIC

CW00400570

Written by Lura Seavey. Updated by Rosanna Gonzalez

Published by Thomas Cook Publishing
A division of Thomas Cook Tour Operations Limited
Company registration no. 1450464 England
The Thomas Cook Business Park, Unit 9, Coningsby Road,
Peterborough PE3 8SB, United Kingdom
Email: books@thomascook.com, Tel: +44 (0) 1733 416477
www.thomascookpublishing.com

Produced by Cambridge Publishing Management Limited
Burr Elm Court, Main Street, Caldecote CB23 7NU

ISBN: 978-1-84157-972-6

First edition © 2006 Thomas Cook Publishing
This second edition © 2008 Thomas Cook Publishing
Text © Thomas Cook Publishing
Maps © 2008 Thomas Cook Publishing/PCGraphics (UK) Limited

Project Editor: Karen Fitzpatrick
Production/DTP: Steven Collins

Printed and bound in Spain by GraphyCems

Cover photography courtesy of Alamy/Tristan Deschamps

CONTENTS

WHAT'S IN YOUR GUIDEBOOK?

Independent authors Impartial up-to-date information from our travel experts who meticulously source local knowledge.

Experience Thomas Cook's 165 years in the travel industry and guidebook publishing enriches every word with expertise you can trust.

Travel know-how Contributions by thousands of staff around the globe, each one living and breathing travel.

Editors Travel-publishing professionals, pulling everything together to craft a perfect blend of words, pictures, maps and design.

You, the traveller We deliver a practical, no-nonsense approach to information, geared to how you really use it.

● *The sun sets over a tranquil Dominican Republic*

INTRODUCTION
Getting to know the Dominican Republic

USA

Dominican
Republic

◎	City
◉	Large Town
○	Small Town
▣	POI
	Motorway
	Main Road
	Minor Road
✈	Airport

Cabrera

Atlantic Ocean

ua

*Bahía
Escocesa*

Portillo

Samaná

5

*Bahía de
Samaná*

Cayo Leventado

as de San Gabriel

Sabana de la Mar

*Parque
Nacional
Los Haïtises*

El Valle

Miches

Nisibón

Monte
Plata

El Seibo

Hato
Mayor

4

San Pedro
de Macorís

4

Higüey

Cortecito

Punta
Cana

ANTO
MINGO

Boca
Chica

La Romana

Juanillo

rio
nal

Las
Américas

3

3

*Parque
Nacional
Submarino
la Caleta*

Isla Catalina

*Parque
Nacional
del Este*

Isla Saona

Caribbean Sea

Dominican
Republic

0   25 km

0   15 miles

Getting to know the Dominican Republic

Jagged mountains peek up between the Caribbean and the Atlantic, surveying the sandy shores and clear blue waters. The sound of music in the distance beckons the visitor closer, while the fresh evening breeze refreshes and invigorates the once-weary traveller.

GEOGRAPHY

Occupying two-thirds of the island of Hispañiola, the Dominican Republic covers an area of 48,734 sq km (18,816 sq miles). The western third of the island is occupied by Haiti, and the Haitian border region is the least developed, and least travelled, area of the Dominican Republic. Haiti itself has had periods of instability in the past, and it is wise to check with the Foreign Commonwealth Office before considering a trip over this border.

Because of the island's formation as a chain of mountains jutting out of the sea, the development of the country has been determined by the landscape. Pico Duarte, which sits in the western region of the country in the Cordillera Central mountain chain, is the island's tallest peak, reaching 3,087 m (10,128 ft). The Cordillera Septentrional is a ridge of lower mountains that defines the northwestern coast, while the Cordillera Oriental forms the eastern end of the island.

Naturally, with all of these mountains come plentiful valleys and streams and rivers to accompany them. The longest river is the Yaque del Norte, extending 296 km (184 miles) long. The Cibao Valley, which is in the basin of the Yaque del Norte, reaps the benefits of the constant feed from the mountains and is known as a fertile region for grain and tobacco farming. There are also many lakes and coastal lagoons dotted around the scenic island.

A good portion of the Dominican Republic landscape is covered in lush greenery, boasting over 5,600 species of plants. But there are also stark contrasts: you could visit a rainforest and its giant trees one day, and on the next, see cacti in the desert. Among native plants are the cashew, coconut, guava and star fruit, as well as the much-coveted mahogany and ebony trees.

LIFESTYLE

Modern Dominicans unfortunately cannot afford the same luxuries as visitors. Traditional industries based on crops such as sugar cane, which used to employ many workers, have given way to less expensive alternatives like corn syrup, leaving many people redundant. Although tourism has brought in other jobs, most hotels are foreign-owned and operated, offering only entry-level positions to locals. For most who live and work on the island, the realities of frequent electrical blackouts and fresh water shortages are a daily problem. However, despite the enormous socio-economic gap, Dominicans are known to be friendly, welcoming hosts.

HISTORY

The Dominican Republic was originally the stronghold of the Taíno Indians until the arrival of Columbus in 1492. He named the island Hispañiola ('Little Spain') and returned with a thousand colonists the following year. The original settlement, La Isabela (see page 63), was abandoned after just a few years and shifted to the present site of Santo Domingo. After numerous pirate attacks, Spain finally ceded the western third of the island to France in 1697. Years of fighting followed until this became the republic of Haiti in 1804. In 1821, the Dominican Republic was formed, although full independence from Spain was not achieved until 1865. From the 1930s, the country was in the grip of the right-wing dictator Rafael Trujillo until his assassination in 1961, when Joaquín Balaguer came to power.

TRADITIONS & RELIGION

Although many aspects of Dominican life have changed in the past few decades, some stand strong as always. Baseball, for one, will always be a strong national pastime. You will find that most towns have a team, and if a game is being played, not much else will be happening! Religion is also important; most Dominicans are Roman Catholic, although there is an underlying influence of old voodoo on the island.

THE BEST OF THE DOMINICAN REPUBLIC

TOP 10 ATTRACTIONS

- **Whale watching in Samaná** During the humpback whale migration and mating season in February and March, whales can be viewed in astounding numbers off the shores of the Samaná Peninsula (see page 43).

- **Historic Santo Domingo** The first city to be founded in the New World, Santo Domingo is filled with a large number of thrilling historic sites (see page 14).

- **Cabarete – windsurfing capital** Cabarete's beach provides perfect winds for year-round windsurfing; kiteboarding is becoming popular too. The town is host to international competitions for both (see pages 46–9).

- **Boca Chica, the non-stop party town** The rum is flowing and the merengue is playing loud, so let your hair down and have some fun in Boca Chica (see page 24)!

- **Diving in Sosúa** Explore the magnificent reefs, swim with bright tropical fish and relax in some of the most picturesque surroundings on the island (see page 53).

- **Isla Saona** This excursion is a must. The adventurous journey to the island by speedboat or catamaran is part of the fun. This island will take your breath away (see pages 83–4).

- **Water rafting and canyoning** This takes place in the Cordillera Central along the country's longest river, the Yaque del Norte in Jarabacoa (see page 76).

- **Golf** The Dominican Republic is a major international golf destination, with some beautiful courses bordered by the ocean. Some of the best courses can be found in Casa de Campo and Punta Cana (see page 37).

- **Dominican Amber Museum** This museum in Puerto Plata displays a unique collection of valuable Dominican amber. The tempting museum shop sells amber jewellery (see page 61).

- **Shopping for Larimar** This unusual light-blue gem with white marbling is the native stone of the Dominican Republic and makes a lovely souvenir. Gemstones are found in several mines across the republic (see page 87).

◗ Aerial view of the beach at Samaná

SYMBOLS KEY

The following is a key to the symbols used throughout this book:

ⓐ address ☎ telephone ⓕ fax ⓦ website address ⓔ email 🕑 opening times
Ⓝ public transport connections ❶ important

Ⓜ metro stop
ⓘ information office
✉ post office
🛍 shopping
🛫 airport
✚ hospital
🛡 police station
🚌 bus station/stop
🚆 railway station
✝ church
❶ numbers denote featured cafés, restaurants & evening venues

○ city
○ large town
○ small town
▪ POI (point of interest)
═ motorway
▬ main road
▬ minor road
▬ railway

RESTAURANT CATEGORIES
Meals are rated according to the following guidelines. Please note, each rating is based on the cost of a main course for one person without drinks.

£ = under $30 **££** = $30–$55 **£££** = over $55

▶ *Santo Domingo is a great place to relax*

RESORTS
Places under the sun

Santo Domingo

At the top of the list of things to see in this exciting city is the area known as the Zona Colonial, where you can find many of the oldest sights of the New World still intact, and the remains of many others. From the 16th-century palace, **Alcázar de Don Diego Colón** to the **Parque Independencia**, where Juan Pablo Duarte and his fellow revolutionaries led the country to freedom against the Haitians, this part of the town is rich in history. After you have explored the old town, there's plenty more to see – modern Santo Domingo has a multitude of great shops, fantastic restaurants and outstanding nightlife.

When visiting the capital, it is hard to miss the 8-km (5-mile) oceanfront stretch known as the **Malecón**. The official street name is Avenida George Washington, and it is lined with an abundance of clubs, hotels, restaurants, bars, and various other places to rest and have a drink. At night it is especially popular with younger visitors. The action doesn't usually begin here until very late in the evening and carries on into the early morning hours. But don't worry if this is too late for you – there is plenty of shopping and food to be found along the main strip of the Zona Colonial during daylight hours.

The **Calle el Conde** in the Zona Colonial is as fast-paced and busy as you would expect a main city street to be, and you will find all the modern conveniences here you need. ATMs (cash machines) and even some fast food chains have moved into the area because of its popularity, and souvenir shops accept credit cards.

There is a tourist office on Isabela la Católica in the Zona Colonial, but English is rarely spoken here. You are advised to ask your hotel concierge or host for information.

THINGS TO SEE & DO (Greater Santo Domingo)

Acuario Nacional (National Aquarium)

Visitors can experience underwater life in a unique way here as they walk through a plexiglass tunnel while sharks and fish swim all around.

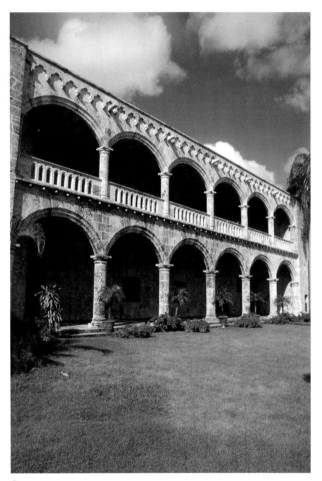

◔ The restored palace, Alcázar de Don Diego Colón

Shallow areas are open for children and adults to have encounters with friendly sea creatures such as turtles.

ⓐ Avenida España 🕾 809 766 1709 🕘 09.30–17.30 Tues–Sun
ⓘ Admission charge

Agua Splash

Especially popular with children, this water park with waterslides and pools is a cooling diversion on a hot day. Weekends can be very crowded with tourists and local families.

ⓐ Avenida España 50, Ensanche Isabelita 🕾 809 766 1927
ⓦ www.aguasplashcaribe.com 🕘 11.00–19.00 Tues–Sun
ⓘ Admission charge

Cuevas De Los Tres Ojos (Caves of the Three Eyes)

A beautiful cave with three clear and bright blue lagoons. One site requires the use of a ferry (at additional charge), and some walking on steep, rocky steps is involved so wear sensible footwear. Set on the east bank of the Ozama River with an inspiring jungle-type atmosphere, it has been the location for many film shoots. The site was also once a very spiritual place for the natives of the island.

ⓐ Avenida Las Americas 🕘 09.30–17.30 ⓘ Admission charge

Faro a Colón (Columbus Lighthouse)

Although this has been quite a controversial structure in many ways due to its cost, location and other problems, it can be stunning when lit and is certainly a landmark of Dominican history. Shaped like a giant cross, the lighthouse was the inflated idea of Joaquin Balaguer during his regime as leader since the 1960s. Although many other places claim the same, the remains of Columbus are supposedly within the walls.

ⓐ Parque Mirador del Este, Avenida Estados Unidos, Villa Duarte
🕾 809 591 1492/809 592 5217 🕘 09.30–17.30 Tues–Sun
ⓘ Admission charge

Jardín Botánico Nacional (Botanical Garden)

Santo Domingo's botanical garden is the largest in the Caribbean. The extensive grounds can be viewed from a small train (ride is included in admission price), or you may walk the gardens by yourself or with a guide. The Japanese garden is a favourite attraction, with a lovely pagoda for shade, and the 300 varieties of orchids found in the remainder of the garden are astounding. The site also attracts many species of birds and other wildlife.

ⓐ Calle República de Colombia esq. Los Próceres, Arroyo Hondo
ⓣ 809 385 0860 ⓒ 09.00–17.30 ⓘ Admission charge

Parque Zoológico Nacional (National Zoo)

A visit to the zoo offers the opportunity to view a strange assortment of creatures up close, such as crocodiles, hyenas and flamingos. The rarest animal that lives at this zoo is Hispañiola's native solenodon, a small, anteater-like rodent that is near extinction and exists nowhere else in the world.

ⓐ Avenida La Vega Real, Arroyo Hondo ⓣ 809 562 3149
ⓒ Daily 09.00–17.00 ⓘ Admission charge

THINGS TO SEE & DO (Central Santo Domingo)

Plaza de la Cultura (The Cultural Plaza) is a complete city block set aside for four museums and a theatre, as detailed in the following entries. Visitors should be aware that they must be dressed appropriately in order to get into any of these museums – no beachwear, shorts, sleeveless shirts or otherwise inappropriate clothing is permitted.

ⓐ Avenida Máximo Gómez and Avenida Dr Pedro Henriquez Ureña

Galeria de Arte Moderno (Modern Art Museum)

Set up to give this century's Dominican artists more prominence, many visitors will be surprised at the wide subject range of this museum.

ⓐ See Plaza de la Cultura ⓣ 809 685 2153 ⓒ 10.00–18.00 Tues–Sun
ⓘ Admission charge

Central Santo Domingo

Museo de Historia Natural (Natural History Museum)

This museum has a planetarium with a laser show about the galaxy.
There are many exhibits that focus on the geology of the country, such
as fossils and larimar (a blue gem of volcanic origin, found only in the
Dominican Republic), and there is a large section explaining exactly what
amber is composed of, as well as how it is formed. Other attractions
include a huge whale skeleton and many of the island's stuffed native
animals on display.

ⓐ See Plaza de la Cultura ⓣ 809 689 0106 ⓛ 10.00–17.00 Tues–Sun
ⓘ Admission charge

Museo de Historia y Geografía (History and Geography Museum)

Here, history aficionados can see relics of past dictator Trujillo, including
a car from his motorcade (filled with bullets) from the day he was
assassinated, or the electric chair once used for torture.

ⓐ See Plaza de la Cultura ⓣ 809 686 6668 ⓛ 09.30–16.30 Tues–Sun
ⓘ Admission charge

Museo del Hombre Dominicano (Museum of Dominican Man)

You need to bypass the first two floors to find the collections in this
museum. Here you will see an extensive collection of Taíno artefacts
including jewellery, weapons, and artwork, such as sculptures of gods.
Other collections include a display on the slave trade and its impact on
the country, and another examines how the mixture of cultures has
affected Roman Catholicism and religion in the country. A popular
exhibit is the model *campesino* house, which shows in great detail the
simplicity of Dominican rural life outside the cities.

ⓐ See Plaza de la Cultura ⓣ 809 687 3622 ⓛ 10.00–17.00 Tues–Sun
ⓘ Admission charge

Teatro Nacional (National Theatre)

This theatre holds performances and other events.

ⓐ See Plaza de la Cultura ⓣ 809 687 3191 ⓛ Tues–Sun, by schedule

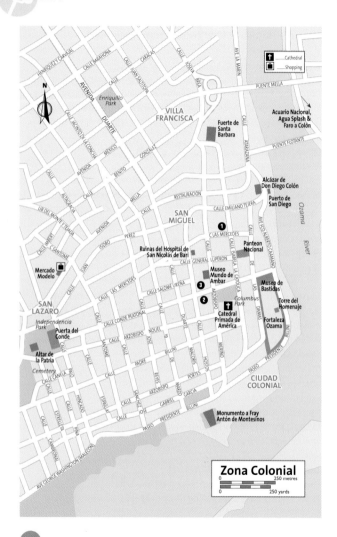

Zona Colonial

0 _____ 250 metres

0 _____ 250 yards

THINGS TO SEE & DO (Zona Colonial)

Alcázar de Don Diego Colón (The Palace of Diego Columbus)
This palace has been fully restored to its former glory after once
falling into such disrepair it was virtually a pile of rubble. During its
initial construction in 1510, not even one nail was used. It was the home
of Diego Colón (Columbus' eldest son) and his family, and was the
country's prominent palace until their departure some six decades later.
ⓐ Plaza de España ⓣ 809 609 5946 ⓛ 09.00–17.00 ❶ Admission charge

Catedral Primada de América (America's First Cathedral)
Reputed to be the first cathedral built in the New World, construction
was begun by Diego Colón in 1514. It has great arching ceilings,
sculptures and paintings. Be sure to wear appropriate clothes,
no shorts or sleeveless shirts.
ⓐ Parque Colón, Calle Arzobispo Meriño ⓛ 09.00–16.00

Museo Mundo de Ambar (Amber World Museum)
Displays and a workshop (see page 90).
ⓐ Arzobispo Meriño 452 ⓣ 809 682 3309
ⓦ www.amberworldmuseum.com ⓛ 09.00–18.00

Puerta del Conde
This historical gate, designed to defend the city from invading armies, is
where the Colonial Zone ends and where the remains of the liberators of
the Dominican Republic are buried.

Ruinas del Hospital de San Nicolás de Bari
(Ruins of the St Nicholas of Bari Hospital)
This site was the first hospital built by the European settlers in the
New World.
ⓐ Calle Hostos and Calle General Luperón

TAKING A BREAK

Pasatiempo Ristorante Pizzería Italiana £ ❶ (see map page 20)
Fantastic pizzas, calzones and other traditional Italian specialities
available here. ⓐ Isabel la Católica 204 ❶ 809 689 4823

Alfatori Restaurant ££ ❷ (see map page 20) International dishes
served in an upmarket environment. Live music is also often a feature.
ⓐ Arzobispo Meriño 115, next to the Catedral Primada de América
(America's First Cathedral) ❶ 809 682 8220 ⓦ www.alfatori.com

Hard Rock Café ££ ❸ (see map page 20) Young and interesting, it's the
biggest one in Latin America ⓐ Calle El Conde 103 ❶ 809 686 7771

CARNIVAL!
Each year, residents of Santo Domingo combine their traditional
pre-Lenten festivities in February with their Independence Day
holiday, making the entire month one long celebration, all
culminating on 27 February to re-create the revolution in 1844 at
the Parque Independencia.

Celebrated every Sunday in February and ending in a huge event
at the end of the month just before Lent, Carnival is full of parades,
parties, dancing and fun for all. Santo Domingo holds one of the
most boisterous and well-known celebrations, drawing in crowds
from all over the world. Residents spend the entire year working
on their artistic and flamboyant costumes. Masks depicting
el Diablo (the devil) are very common, as well as bright and
festive dresses.

The city also hosts several other festivals throughout the year,
including the Latin Music Festival in September (every two years),
the Merengue Festival in July and August, and the Restoration
Festival in August (see Festivals & events, page 108).

Mesón de la Cava ££ ④ (see map page 18) Fine international cuisine, along with lovely atmosphere. ⓐ Avenida Mirador del Sur 1 ⓣ 809 533 2818

Mix Food to Share ££ ⑤ (see map page 18) International and creative food in a pleasant ambience. ⓐ Calle Gustavo Mejía Ricart 69, Torre Washington ⓣ 809 472 0100

AFTER DARK

The 8-km (5-mile) stretch of beachfront known as the **Malecón** (see page 14) is a collection of nightclubs, bars, restaurants and assorted shops to fit just about anyone's taste. ⓐ Avenida George Washington ⓛ Lively late at night until 02.00

Alta Copa Wine and Lounge ⑥ (see map page 18) Good place to go for a drink and a dance. ⓐ Calle Pedro A. Bobea 6 ⓣ 809 532 6405

Discoteca Jet Set Club ⑦ (see map page 18) A traditional place to go and dance. ⓐ Avenida Independencia 2253 ⓣ 809 535 4145

Discoteca Jubilee ⑧ (see map page 18) A good place to dance the night away. ⓐ Renaissance Jaragua Night Club and Casino, Avenida George Washington 367 ⓣ 809 533 215/809 221 2222

Boca Chica

Still a lovely spot, this once-coveted location has, in recent years, earned a reputation for being host to one long party. The city has a lively and carefree atmosphere and there is always the sound of very loud music playing somewhere. The sea is a radiant blue and there is plenty of fun to be had for everyone.

Boca Chica is about 30 minutes drive from Santo Domingo, 10 minutes beyond Las Américas Airport. Weekends here are especially crowded, when people who live in Santo Domingo make the short 25-km (16-mile) trip to swim at the perfect beach. The shallow waters here are the biggest attraction, extending at wading height far enough to walk to an island.

Boca Chica has not always been the wild-child offshoot of the capital city. As a resort town, it was once quite exclusive and the holiday favourite for wealthy visitors from abroad. Long before that, the native Taíno appreciated the area's natural beauty as well; after an extensive archaeological dig, this same spot was found to have been a major Taíno centre.

If you want to join in on the seaside merengue and rum, remember that daytime is far safer than the night-time for travellers here. Tourists of both sexes are likely to be approached by prostitutes and drug dealers in all parts of the city when joining in festivities after dark.

THINGS TO SEE & DO

Playa Boca Chica

The beach is divided roughly into three sections, with the eastern section restricted to those staying at a beachfront resort. The central section of the beach is the most lively party zone, and can be accessed at the end of Calle Hungria. You will find everything you need beachside here, including food, drink, and light shopping. The western end of the beach is quieter and usually more suitable for families. The food found here is served in local-type shacks.

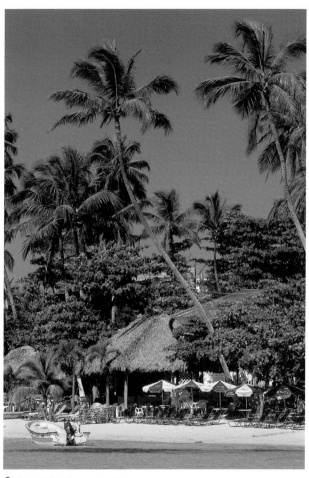

◗ *The lively beach at Boca Chica*

⬤ *Divers can explore a sunken ship and the surrounding coral reef*

EXCURSION
Parque Nacional Submarino la Caleta

Now a coral-reef in the making, the main attraction at this national park is the scuttled treasure hunt ship, *The Hickory*. At its deepest, the protected area reaches 180 m (590 ft), making it highly accessible to divers who want to explore the open hull and tropical undersea life. The park also includes a small museum of Taino artefacts. There is no official diving service set up, so making prior arrangements with your guide is highly recommended, rather than choosing one of the many fishermen who are looking to make extra money.

ⓐ Route 66, 22 km (14 miles) east of Santo Domingo

TAKING A BREAK

You will not be hard pressed to find either fast food or traditional Dominican fare virtually anywhere along the beach and in the tourist areas of the city.

La Criolla £ Highly recommended for traditional Dominican food. Often busy, even in the wee hours of the morning. ⓐ Calle Duarte 🕒 24 hours a day

Neptuno's ££ Known for its extraordinary fresh seafood, it is best to hire a taxicab to bring you to this restaurant. ⓐ Calle Duarte 12 🕿 809 523 4703 🅦 www.neptunos.com.do 🕒 Daily for brunch and dinner ❶ Reservations recommended

El Pelicano ££ This restaurant by the sea specialises in seafood. ⓐ Calle Duarte 1, next to Hotel Oasis Hamaca 🕿 809 523 4611 ext. 830, reservations 809 523 9494 🕒 11.00–24.00

San Pedro de Macoris

If you didn't know any better, this old sugar cane area might seem somewhat run-down. In fact it is home to several of the world's most productive Major League Baseball training camps and has produced many incredible athletes. Despite the economic struggles that San Pedro has faced after losing the sugar cane industry and being hit by ruthless hurricanes, *béisbol* (baseball) still keeps spirits high.

The high poverty and homelessness rate in San Pedro may deter some from visiting, but the people are determined and make the best of their home. There is more than just baseball for the residents to be proud of. Here you will find a wider range of cultural backgrounds than in many other places, and as a result the festivals and parades have their own certain spice. The architecture has a heavy Victorian influence as this was the period of the city's greatest wealth gained from sugar.

PLAY BALL!

Baseball aficionados won't want to miss San Pedro, and should look into booking from late November to February in order to catch the training season. Major League teams from North America and Japanese teams have their own training grounds, and also use the local team's stadium for practice. It was this very city that raised the baseball stars Sammy Sosa, Tony Fernandez and Alfonso Soriano.

Recruiters from all the major teams also make this their home base, and as a result this is a central place for games to be played so that local talent can strut its stuff. It is considered certain success for a young man to attain a minor league contract, so many boys are groomed towards that goal from an early age.

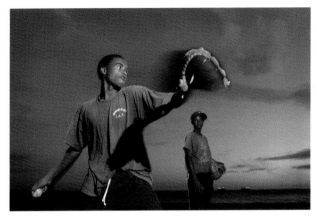

◓ *Baseball is more than just a popular pastime in San Pedro*

THINGS TO SEE & DO

Estadio Tetelo Vargas (Tetelo Vargas Stadium)

This ball field is the pride and joy of San Pedro's home team, Las Estrellas Orientales (the Eastern Stars). It is not uncommon to find Major League players working out here during the day, and the scouts are always hanging around looking for the next local superstar. Schedules for games can be found in newspapers as far away as Santo Domingo. Games are usually played in the evening.

ⓐ Avenida Circunvalación & Carretera Mella

George Bell Mansion

Baseball fans will want to stop by this huge monument to one of the city's first great Major League baseball heroes, built for him after he made his fame in the United States.

ⓐ Avenida 27 de Febrero

Iglesia San Pedro Apóstol

This church is simple yet elegant in appearance, with a whitewashed exterior, three rows of pews and a mahogany altar. It was built in 1911 and the bell tower that rises so close to the shoreline somehow survived even Hurricane Georges in 1998.

ⓐ Avenida Charro and Independencia

Malecón

Although not anything like the Malecón of Santo Domingo, this is still a lively place where visitors are guaranteed to find plenty of local food shacks, vendors and activity. The views are beautiful, but swimming here is not such a good idea – pollution left from the city's industrial days is still an issue.

ⓐ Avenida Gaston F Deligne (which begins at Howard Johnson Hotel Macorix)

TAKING A BREAK

Much like other towns, there are often plenty of street vendors offering traditional foods wherever people congregate, especially along the beach. If you are looking for more upmarket cuisine, your best bet is to eat at your hotel.

Casa La Esquina Caliente £ One of the only pizza places in town that isn't a foreign-owned chain. ⓐ Avenida Circunvalación 8 ⓣ 809 529 0120

Mi Sitio £ Casual, home-style atmosphere. ⓐ Avenida Malecón
ⓣ 809 529 8373 ⓛ Lunch and dinner, closed Mon

Pica Pollo La Ceniza £ Fried chicken is the speciality here.
ⓐ Calle F A Caamaño 40 ⓣ 809 246 4038 ⓛ Daily from 12.00

Pittsburgh Pirates £ Baseball-themed American-fare restaurant.
ⓐ Calle Rufino Linares ⓣ 809 246 5712

El Taquito £ Traditional Dominican, fast-food fare. ❷ Calle Sánchez 20
❶ 809 529 2253 ❹ Daily until late

AFTER DARK

Exótica Bar Café Typical, small nightclub atmosphere. ❷ Calle R Mota
❶ 809 529 9392

Restaurant Disco Terraza El Catedrático A restaurant that features music
and dancing. ❷ Avenida Circunvalación 20-A ❶ 809 529 6887

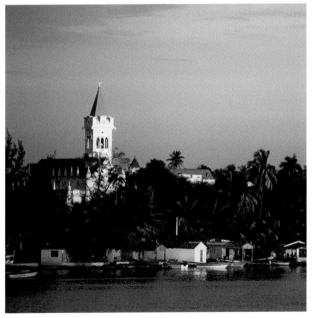

◯ *San Pedro de Macoris has produced many incredible athletes*

La Romana

La Romana is perhaps one of the country's most exclusive areas, made famous as the site of Lisa Marie Presley and Michael Jackson's wedding. Once a town made wealthy by the sugar cane industry, its main source of revenue is now tourism. The city is renowned for attracting celebrities from around the world, many of whom own private villas nearby.

Exclusivity and very tight security are to be expected here, since a large section of the town is owned by the **Casa de Campo** resort. Guests there wear bracelets that act as their pass within the resort which is so big they are advised to use a car just to get around the grounds. The **Parque Central** (Central Park) in La Romana is a lovely place to visit to see some nice homes in the bright and festive colours that have become a trademark in the country. In the evening you will find fewer tourists and more local residents relaxing in the park, taking in the atmosphere and meeting friends. One block north you will find the **Mercado Modelo**, where prices on local arts and crafts may be slightly lower than in the other shops in town.

THINGS TO SEE & DO

Altos de Chavón

Often considered a shopping complex, this high-end tourist haven contains enough to occupy a visitor for at least an entire day. The decor is not quite Caribbean – it has an old-fashioned, rather contrived, European look, perhaps the result of too much stucco and artificial ageing techniques. However, in addition to a wide range of shops, you will find plenty of good restaurants and evening entertainment.

Amphitheatre

If you love music, you will want to find out about the shows being offered in the 5,000-seat amphitheatre, including the annual Jazz Festival. This open-air stadium has been host to both modern and classic greats such as Shakira, Julio Iglesias, Frank Sinatra and Carlos Santana.

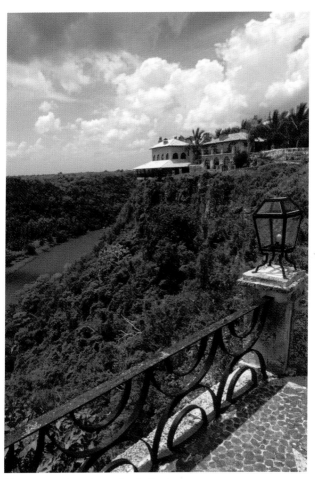

◆ *A view from the exclusive Altos de Chavón*

Casa de Campo

This pleasant resort of luxury villas is a short drive east of town. Non-guests are allowed to visit this resort, but arrangements should be made first if you are interested in using any of the facilities. Casa de Campo offers horse riding, diving, entertainment, and a full array of outdoor activities. Three 18-hole golf courses and a skeet (clay pigeon) shooting course are open to the public with no prior arrangement needs to be made.

ⓣ 809 523 3333 ⓦ www.casadecampo.com.do

Church of St Stanislaus

Because if its popularity, this grand edifice is not as peaceful a retreat as one might hope, but it is well worth a stop to enjoy the architecture and views. The church's pride is the fountain of the four lions.

ⓐ Main Plaza ⓛ Mass 17.00 Sat & Sun; church open when Mass not taking place

Rancho Cumayasa Eco

This resort offers non-staying guests the option of buying day passes, which include lunch, a one-hour horseback ride, access to paddleboats and admission to the resort's popular children's attraction 'Hurricane House'.

ⓐ Highway 4 ⓣ 809 556 1606 ⓘ Admission charge

Museo Arqueológico Regional (Regional Museum of Archaeology)

This simple museum displays Taíno artefacts and is a welcome break from the surrounding bustle. Exhibits are mainly from the personal collections of the archaeologist Samuel Pion.

ⓐ Altos de Chavón ⓣ 809 523 8554 ⓛ Daily 09.00–20.00 ⓘ No admission charge

TAKING A BREAK

Pica Pollo La Esperanza £ Traditional, Dominican fried chicken.
ⓐ H P Quezada 132 ⓣ 809 556 3841

SHOPPING

La Tienda Literally meaning 'the store', this is an upmarket handicraft boutique. Much of what is on sale is tailored to the tastes and needs of American and European visitors. ⓐ Altos de Chavón ⓣ 809 523 3333 ext. 5398 ⓛ Daily 09.00–20.00

The Principal Gallery, the Rincón Gallery and the Loggia Gallery
These three gallery spaces are connected, and each offers the chance to view contemporary art from around the world. In addition to fine art, some speciality crafts are also sold on consignment here and it is a good place to find high-quality (albeit overpriced) Dominican handiwork. ⓐ Altos de Chavón ⓣ 809 523 8470 ⓛ Daily 09.30–19.00 ❶ Exhibits change monthly

Everett Designs Named for the designer and artisan Bill Everett, this jewellery shop is worth a mention for its gorgeous collection. ⓐ Altos de Chavón ⓣ 809 523 8331 ⓛ 10.00–19.00 Tues–Sat

Pizzería Alondra £ Privately owned and great for a quick bite. ⓐ F del C Márquez 88 ⓣ 809 550 4115 ⓛ Daily 11.00–23.00

Giacosa Restaurante £££ A stunning, rustic setting, with live piano music, a full bar and a patio overlooking the Chavón River. Full international wine selection suits the tasty, sophisticated Italian menu. ⓐ Altos de Chavón ⓣ 809 523 8466/8373 ⓦ www.giacosa.com.do ⓛ Daily from 11.00

AFTER DARK

Estudio 2000 Discoteca A low-key dance club with a bar that is usually packed. ⓐ Avenida Santa Rosa 63 ⓣ 809 813 0481 ⓛ Daily from 22.00

Intimo Piano Bar A small bar with a cosy atmosphere. ⓐ Calle 1ra 67, Los Colonos ⓣ 809 813 4198 ⓛ Daily from 18.00

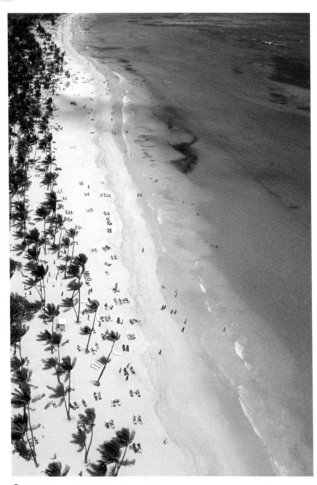

◆ *Punta Cana, a beach-lover's paradise*

Punta Cana

Heavily influenced by the large number of European travellers, Punta Cana is mostly made up of resort hotels lined up along the beach. In contrast to some other resort locations, there is less segregation between tourists and locals here – that is to say, since there is no original town that was overrun by a giant hotel, the establishments are not obsessed with keeping locals out of their tennis courts and off their beaches. Punta Cana sits at the eastern end of Hispañiola and is most revered for its perfect, soft white sand.

The resort-made beach zone is popular with Latin Americans and Spanish as well as celebrities – Julio Iglesias often stays in his villa here. Punta Cana has its own airport, or can easily be accessed by bus from other regions. This area is packed with activities, ranging from casinos and nightclubs to plenty of watersports and relaxing time for sunbathing. It is a good town for those who prefer to have all amenities at their fingertips and do not want the hassle of looking about for something to do. There is always a party and never a dull moment along the beach, yet the town is not known for being rowdy or rough.

For those who are just passing through and would like to get a glimpse of the well-known beaches without booking at a mega-hotel or perhaps as a break from the frenzy of the high life, there is one public access beach. Located at **Cortecito**, it is far more relaxed than the rest of the area. Here you will find local beachgoers and adventurous Europeans taking a dip to cool off. If you are looking for a truly rustic getaway, try the little fishing town of **Juanillo**, 6 km (4 miles) south of Punta Cana.

THINGS TO SEE & DO

Diving

Scuba Caribe SA Five locations in Punta Cana offering lessons and rentals for beginners as well as experienced scuba divers.
ⓐ Carretera Friusa 1 ⓣ 809 221 1336/809 552 6249

Horse riding

Rancho RN-23 With over 100 horses to choose from at three ranches, the operation offers guided tours throughout the area.

ⓐ Arena Gorda ⓣ 809 552 1529/809 552 1670

Outback Jungle Safari

This day-long tour may not be what many expect from its exotic name. Tour operators pick you up from your hotel and will spend the day showing guests around the countryside by truck, exposing visitors to the real lives of the Dominican people. Some of the places visited include a school where visitors can speak to the local students, and you also get the chance to visit a market, and see how vanilla and coffee are produced. Meals and drinks (including rum) are included in the price of the day, plus a siesta in a hammock.

ⓐ Plaza Turisol, Local 7, Avenida Luperón ⓣ 809 244 4886 (north coast) or 809 552 0665 ⓦ www.outback-safaris.com ⓘ Admission charge; tours by booking; ages 12 & over

TAKING A BREAK

Hard Rock Café ££ Situated in the Palma Real Shopping Village, this café offers the brand's usual rock atmosphere, American fare and a shop.

ⓐ Cortecito 57 ⓣ 809 552 0594 ⓛ Daily 11.30–02.00

Capitán Cook £££ This place specialises in grilled seafood and has lovely beachside views. ⓐ Marina el Cortecito ⓣ 809 552 0645/809 221 1828

AFTER DARK

Bavaro Disco This European-style disco with a state-of-the-art sound system is known for its loud music and scantily clad clientele, and is one of the most popular nightclubs in the area. ⓐ Bávaro Barcelo Beach, Golf & Casino Resort ⓣ 809 686 5797 ⓛ 23.00–05.00 ⓘ Admission charge for those not staying at the resort

Samaná Peninsula & Santa Barbara de Samaná

When Christopher Columbus discovered this Caribbean paradise in 1493, he described it as 'the fairest land on the face of the earth'. With its coconut-covered mountains and colourful coral reefs, this entrancing region offers much for beach lovers and those seeking more adventurous exploits.

For many travellers, the Samaná Peninsula is the ideal retreat. With a setting no less perfect than the other resorts, this area's white sands and turquoise waters have more space and more to see. The region has become well known for its whale watching, especially for those who like to view the humpback during its winter migration. The Samaná Peninsula is also home to **Parque Nacional los Haïtises** (see page 80), one of the most visited wildlife sanctuaries in the country.

Natural wonders are revered by the residents of the peninsula, and there has been a significant effort in this area in particular to encourage the idea of sustainable tourism. In this way, visitors and Dominicans can work together to maintain the land and the things the tourists have come to see, so that the industry will not destroy itself. Many farmers and locals on the peninsula are guides (also known as *paradas*) and craftspeople who will share the natural wonders of the landscape at an absurdly small fee. An astounding number of gorgeous waterfalls are among some of the most popular destinations.

Not all of the Samaná Peninsula is made up of small towns and jungles, however. The city of **Santa Barbara de Samaná** (known as Samaná) has its own share of lively bustle, especially along its Malecón. Offering its share of restaurants and nightlife, it allows the naturalist the opportunity to unwind after a day of hiking with some merengue and rum. Since this well-protected port is the central point for the bay's whale watching industry, it becomes quite busy from January through to March while the whale population is high off its coast. During these months, the pace picks up significantly at the clubs along the Malecón, and those planning to visit should make reservations well in advance.

Santa Barbara
de Samaná

DIVE HOTSPOTS

Cabo Cabrón Known as a spot where divers might hear the eerie songs of migrating whales.

La Catedral An enormous, underwater cave that has created an air pocket.

Plaza Monica Advanced divers can reach this reef – 30 m (100 ft) down – that houses large, bright sea life.

The Tower 50 m (165 ft) of this 55-m (180-ft) mountain is under water, rich with amazing sea life.

THINGS TO SEE & DO

La Churcha (First African Wesleyan Methodist Church of Samaná)

This historic building, brought to the island by the English as a mission attempt by the Methodists in 1823, is now a makeshift museum about the area's slave trade and local African culture.

ⓐ Calle Santa Barbara and Calle Duarte ⓒ 09.00–18.00

Diving

Dive Samaná This outfit offers rentals and transportation to many great diving locations in the area.

ⓐ Casa Marina Bay Resort ⓣ 809 538 0210 ⓒ Daily ⓘ Admission charge

Stellina Dive Centre Coordinates dive trips to both popular and little-known spots in the region.

ⓐ Hotel Cacao Beach, Las Terrenas ⓣ 809 240 6000
ⓘ Excursions by reservation

Waterfalls

Waterfalls are usually toured with the aid of guides known as *paradas*. They may offer a meal or snack, show you crafts or a product that they and family members have made to sell, or simply offer to bring you to your destination. You may also choose to walk there yourself, but the trails can be difficult and steep and the fees for the *paradas'* ride on a horse or mule are very small in relation, so their services are recommended. You can also arrange to have a traditional meal waiting for you on your return.

Watersports

Moto Marina Club This club offers rentals and instruction in snorkelling, kayaking, or paddleboating, as well as round-trip transportation services to Cayo Levantado.

ⓐ Avenida la Marina (Malecón) 3 ➊ 809 538 2302
ⓔ motomarina@yahoo.com ➋ Daily by schedule

🔺 *Enjoy the natural wonders of the Samaná Peninsula*

Salto de Limón (Limón Waterfall) This is the best-known waterfall in the region, with a drop of 46 m (150 ft) into a deep pool with lush, tropical surroundings. All trails that lead to the falls are maintained by the Association for Community Ecotourism of Salto del Limón (ACESAL). Trails sprout off from the road between Las Terrenas and Samaná, and along here you will find the many guides offering their services. Some of the more established *paradas* include Parada La Familia, Parada Ismael, Parada Santi, Parada Nega and Parada La Manzana. Many who are not listed are respected guides as well.

Whale watching

From mid-January to late March, several thousand humpback whales make their way to the temperate waters around the island, where the females give birth and the yearly mating takes place. Hopeful bull whales show off to prospective mates, and make a great show for the whale watchers, too. It is an impressive sight, and an excellent opportunity to witness the interactions and rituals of these giants of the deep.

Moto Marina Whale Watching Tours Multilingual staff provide an accompanying narration on boat excursions to watch the humpback migration. Moto Marina also offers round-trip transportation services to Cayo Levantado.

🅐 Avenida la Marina (Malecón) 3 ☎ 809 538 2302
🅔 motomarina@yahoo.com 🕒 Whale watching tours operate daily 15 Jan–25 Mar

Whale Samaná & Victoria Marine Operated by Kim Bedall, known as one of the pioneers of the local whale watching industry. There are two departure points, operating from 15 January–20 March:
🅐 Avenida la Marina (Malecón) ☎ 809 538 2494 🕒 Two tours daily, departing 09.00 & 13.30 and 🅐 Cayo Levantado 🕒 Two tours daily, departing 09.30 & 14.00

◆ *Watching whales off the Samaná coast is an unforgettable experience*

TAKING A BREAK

Café de Paris £ ❶   Excellent pizzas, operated by French owners in a relaxed atmosphere. ⓐ Avenida la Marina (Malecón) 6 ❶ 809 538 2257 🕐 10.00–24.00

Camilo Malecón £ ❷   Traditional Dominican meals, right on the water. ⓐ Avenida la Marina (Malecón) 🕐 10.00–23.00

Restaurante Chino £ ❸   Typical Chinese food for take-away or dining in. ⓐ T Chasereaux ❶ 809 538 2215 🕐 14.00–24.00

La Hacienda £–££ ❹   Known for steaks and French cuisine in a lovely outdoor café setting. ⓐ E de Leon 6 ❶ 809 538 2383 🕐 Daily for lunch and dinner

AFTER DARK

Anyeli Café Club £ ❺   Full bar also offering light food and music. ⓐ Calle Principal 25 ❶ 809 538 0053

La Loba £ ❻   With more local clientele, a laid-back atmosphere and large crowds every night. ⓐ Avenida F de Rosario Sánchez (C5) 🕐 21.00–04.00 ❶ Cover charge

Naomi ££ ❼   Techno-mix club with some Latin music. ⓐ E de Leon 4 🕐 23.00–05.00

Rancho Allegre ££ ❽   Popular venue featuring outdoor dancing to traditional Dominican merengue music. ⓐ Avenida la Marina (Malecón) 🕐 22.00–04.00

Cabarete

Just 20 km (12 miles) from Puerto Plata Airport, this town has become a mecca for windsurfers and kiteboarders. Its white sand beaches combined with near-perfect breezes create ideal conditions for both the first-time windsurfer and the expert watersports enthusiast. The nightlife is equally exciting, with plenty of restaurants and clubs to choose from right along the waterfront. Almost all of the town's action happens along the Calle Principal, or Carretera 5, and the beach it runs parallel to, and it serves as a starting point for many of the region's adventurous excursions, such as hiking and canyoning. Cabarete is most popular with the young and active crowd.

The best time for the novice windsurfer to hit the waves in Cabarete is in the morning, when the breezes are lighter and the water is calmer. One might also feel less self-conscious during the earlier hours when trying to learn the ropes, since the wind picks up as the day progresses and the beach begins to fill with people. Spectators come to watch the more experienced windsurfers, who take full advantage of the trade winds that blow in late in the day.

Kiteboarding is the newest sport to hit the waves, and is popular with young people for its flexibility and stunts. Cabarete is filled with plenty of shops that offer instruction and rentals, and has recently become host to yearly international kiteboarding championships, where spectators can watch some amazing feats performed on the water, including jumps and flips that could never be accomplished with windsurfing.

Cabarete Bay is formed by a barrier coral reef and is a popular destination for surfers and divers. Regrettably the reefs have been damaged by deforestation of upland regions and overfishing has also caused a decline in the environment. But many fishermen now work in tourist hotels, taking pressure off the threatened reefs.

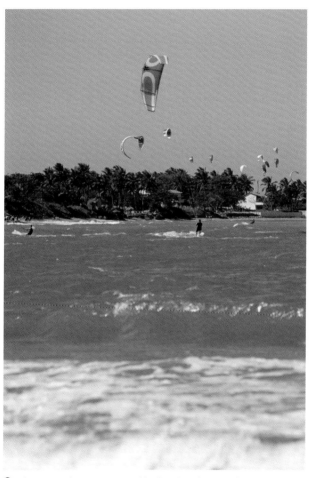

Cabarete now hosts international kiteboarding championships

THINGS TO SEE & DO

Diving
Hippocampo Dive Centre Individual and group diving classes for beginners and those who need to touch up on skills are offered, as well as a good selection of rentals and equipment for sale.
ⓐ Calle Principal (Carretera 5), next to TropiCaña Club Hotel
ⓣ 809 571 0956

Soficap This company offers diving equipment rentals and instruction.
ⓐ Calle Principal (Carretera 5) ⓣ 809 571 0280 ⓛ Daily by appointment

Hiking and adventure tours
Iguana Mama A nationally recognised group of naturalists and guides who offer hiking opportunities to Mount Isabela and Pico Duarte, as well as mountain bike rentals and tours, cultural tours, canyoning and rafting trips, diving instruction and horse riding.
ⓐ Calle Principal 74 (Carretera 5) ⓣ 809 571 0908/571 0228
ⓦ www.iguanamama.com

Parque Nacional El Choco (El Choco National Park)
One of the destinations of Iguana Mama and other local tour operators, the park is best viewed with a guide to truly appreciate its treasures and avoid becoming lost in its maze of jungles, caves and lagoons mapped out by poorly marked paths.

Home to thousands of birds, Parque Nacional El Choco is a stunning place where visitors can see hills that were once undersea coral reefs and visit underground pools in caves that still boast Taíno petroglyphs. The park used to be called the Area Protegida Cabarete y Goleta, named for its two lagoons.
ⓐ Callejón de la Loma ⓛ 09.00–17.00 Mon–Fri ⓘ Entrance fee

Kiteboarding
Caracol Kiteboarding Center Operated by champion windsurfer and kiteboarder Laurel Eastman, this school offers classes for everyone, from

beginner and intermediate, to even the experienced kitesurfer.
🅐 Urbanización Olas de Oro 1 at the Aparthotel Caracol 🕿 809 571 0680
🅦 www.laureleastman.com 🕒 Daily

Dare2Fly Offers kiteboarding equipment rentals and there are also lessons for beginners.
🅐 Office at Calle Principal 1 (Carretera 5); lessons at Kitexcite Beach
🕿 809 571 0787/0805 🕒 Daily ❶ Rental fees

Kitexcite These kiteboarding lessons offer a unique system of radio communication within helmets so the instructors can give immediate feedback while you are on the water. You can also enjoy paragliding lessons which offer an equally thrilling experience in light or even no wind conditions.
🅐 Kitexcite Beach 🕿 809 571 9509/9732 🕒 Daily for lessons, 09.00–17.00 for phone enquiries

Windsurfing
Vela/Spinout Highly regarded windsurfing outfitter that offers equipment rentals with optional insurance and classes.
🅐 Calle Principal 1 (Carretera 5), same location as Dare2Fly office (see above) 🕿 809 571 0787/0805 ❶ Free windsurfing clinics offered daily; lessons by appointment

TAKING A BREAK

The heavy influx of European expats to the area has had a wonderful influence on the culinary selection available to visitors. Many of the town's restaurants are owned and operated by Germans, British, French, Swiss, Italians and others, all of whom contribute to one of the greatest varieties you will find in the country.

Cabarete Blud £ This informal place is open for light meals and snacks.
🅐 Calle Principal 30 (Carretera 5) 🕿 809 571 9714 🕒 10.00–22.00

�â—Ź *Cabarete offers excellent windsurfing opportunities*

Comedor Hebrero £ Fried chicken and other fast food to eat in or take away. ⓐ Carretera C Sabaneta 180, off Calle Principal (Carretera 5) ⓣ 809 571 0712 ⓛ 12.00–23.00

Extreme Restaurant £ Specialises in Asian dishes with mixed menu and buffet. ⓐ Calle Principal (Carretera 5) ⓣ 809 571 0880 ⓛ Daily for breakfast, lunch and dinner

Panadería Repisteria Dick £ Pastries and breads, fresh squeezed juices, and coffee. ⓐ Calle Principal (Carretera 5) ⓣ 809 571 0612 ⓛ Daily 05.00–12.00

La Pizzería De Cabarete £ A typical pizzeria, conveniently located in the centre of town. ⓐ Calle Principal (Carretera 5) ⓣ 809 571 0888 ⓛ Daily 12.00–02.00

El Tiguerre £ A truly authentic Dominican experience, just outside of town. ⓐ Callejón de la Loma ⓛ Lunch only

Las Brisas £–££ Decent food and very popular dance club serving up local music and European techno beats. ⓐ Calle Principal (Carretera 5) ⓣ 809 571 0614 ⓛ Lunch and dinner; bar and club open until 05.00

Caña Tropical ££ International cuisine specialising in fresh seafood, with a wide variety of music including reggae, soul and jazz. ⓐ Calle Principal and Calle Iguana Mama ⓣ 809 571 0101/499 1049 ⓛ Lunch & dinner until 02.00 ⓘ Happy hour 24.00–01.00 every Friday

Casa del Pescador ££ A romantic setting on the beach, serving the day's catch of seafood. ⓐ Calle Principal (Carretera 5) ⓛ 18.00–24.00

Lax ££ A bar and nightclub named for its relaxed atmosphere and general philosophy. It also serves breakfast, lunch and dinner and

specialises in sushi. ⓐ Calle Principal (Carretera 5) ⓣ 809 571 0042
ⓛ 24 hours a day

Ocean Taste Restaurant ££ Seafood so fresh that you may have
snorkelled past it earlier in the day. ⓐ Calle Principal (Carretera 5)
ⓣ 809 571 0430 ⓛ Daily for lunch and dinner

Vento ££ Italian restaurant in a great, central location.
ⓐ Calle Principal 39 (Carretera 5) ⓣ 809 571 0977/805 3377
ⓔ vento@cabareterestaurants.com ⓛ Evenings only

Miro's £££ Miro's offers an expensive but excellent imported wine
selection to accompany fine seafood with a Mediterranean flair.
The restaurant walls act as a gallery for up-and-coming artists.
ⓐ Calle Principal (Carretera 5) ⓣ 809 571 0888 ⓛ 11.00–13.00 &
19.00–24.00

⬤ *The last rays set on the beach at Cabarete*

Sosúa

The charming divers' hotspot of Sosúa was founded as a refugee settlement for about 600 German Jews escaping from the Nazi persecution during World War II. Although it was an attempt to make himself look better after a mass slaughter of Haitians on his own island, Dominican dictator Rafael Trujillo was one of the few leaders at the time who allowed Jewish refugees to freely come to his country. The group developed the land, most notably creating a dairy farming industry, and are known for their fine smoked meats. Despite the country's overwhelming percentage of Roman Catholics, the townspeople of Sosúa have never been met with discrimination. This has given the town a certain draw for Europeans and lends to its continental ambience.

In addition to its international flair, Sosúa is regarded as a growing centre for watersports, especially diving. Its picturesque and inviting beach perfectly resembles a crescent moon, and is tipped with rock structures that extend out into the sea. Surfers and sunbathers enjoy this secluded area, and there are plenty of places to go sailing or jet-skiing.

Sosúa is a divers' paradise, and is certainly the place to go if you are looking for some spectacular dive sites. The waters around the town boast some incredible coral reefs and ocean life that can be easily accessed. Many dive spots are suitable for both beginners and experts, with several levels of treasure to uncover. One of the most fascinating spots is the sunken cargo ship *Zingara*, which plummeted to a depth of 36 m (118 ft). Even here, the less experienced can explore the shallow reef wall above and enjoy the fan corals and tube sponges that make it their home.

THINGS TO SEE & DO

Casino Playa Chiquita

Full-service casino offering 96 gaming machines and seven gaming tables. Also on the premises are a gift shop, restaurant, swimming pool,

nightclub and full amenities to keep guests busy and spending their money.

ⓐ Isabel la Católica ❶ 809 571 3416 ❷ 24 hours a day

Columbus Aquaparque

Large water park equipped with a wide range of rides to satisfy the swimmers, as well as shops, restaurants and bars to keep content those who like to stay dry.

ⓐ Playa Sosúa ❶ 809 571 2642/2254 ❾ www.aguasosua.com
❷ 10.00–18.00 ❶ Admission charge

Diving

Dolphin Underwater Adventure ⓐ Playa Sosúa 45 ❶ 809 571 0842
Escuela de Buceo Eurodive ⓐ Ayuntamiento 44 ❶ 809 571 1093
ⓔ eurodive@verizon.net.do
Northern Coast Aquasports ⓐ Avenida Pedro Clisante 8 ❶ 809 571 1028
Northern Coast Diving ⓐ Avenida Pedro Clisante 8 ❶ 809 571 1028
❾ www.northerncoastdiving.com
Scuba Caribe SA ⓐ Calle Dr A Martínez ❶ 809 571 1014

FunCity Action Park

Go-carts, bumper cars, grand prix and more, plus a special kiddie section for ages 2–8. Food and beverages on site, and shuttle services to and from Sosúa and other nearby towns provided.

ⓐ Carretera Puerto Plata, Km 5 ❶ 809 320 1031
❾ www.funcity-gocarts.com ❷ Daily ❶ Admission charge

Museo Judío Sosúa (Hebrew Colony Museum)

Set up by the refugees during World War II, this museum features exhibits on local Jewish colonies.

ⓐ Calle Dr A Martínez and Calle Dr Rosen ❶ 809 571 1386
❷ 09.00–13.00 & 14.00–16.00 Mon–Fri; call ahead for groups
❶ Admission charge

TAKING A BREAK

Comedor Pica Pollo el Nuevo Día £ ❶ Traditional Dominican fried chicken spot. ⓐ General G Luperón 5 ☎ 809 571 3823 🕐 10.00–22.00

Restaurant Pizzeria Da'Alberto £ ❷ Typical pizzeria with in-house dining. ⓐ Calle Dr A Martinez 53 ☎ 809 571 2069 🕐 10.00–23.00

Tainobeach £–££ ❸ This restaurant and bar serves up seafood, steaks and pizza in a funky round hut. ⓐ El Batey, next to Casa Marina Beach Hotel ☎ 809 571 2434 🕐 Daily for lunch and dinner; bar open until 04.00

La Puntilla de Piergiorgio ££ ❹ Specialising in fresh seafood and Italian entrées. Enjoys great views over the bay. ⓐ Calle La Puntilla (at the Piergiorgio Palace Hotel) ☎ 809 571 2626/2215 🕐 12.00–23.00

AFTER DARK

Voodoo Lounge ❺ This disco declares itself 'a step up', although it still draws in a heavy drinking crowd. ⓐ Calle Pedro Clisante, by the Sosúa Bay Hotel ☎ 809 571 3559 🕐 17.00–05.00

DIVE SITES

If you're an experienced diver or you're learning but want to get the most of your trip, here are the places to ask about:

Airport Wall Considered one of the best spots, this 24-m (79-ft) deep area has several caves and elkhorn coral.

Garden of Los Charamicos Large sponges and bright fan corals adorn this site, reaching a maximum depth of 24 m (79 ft).

Paradise Reef Novices will enjoy the bright coral reef at about 12 m (39 ft), while experts can visit octopus and squid at 32 m (105 ft).

Pyramids A beautiful result of erosion, go 15 m (49 ft) down through and between the corals.

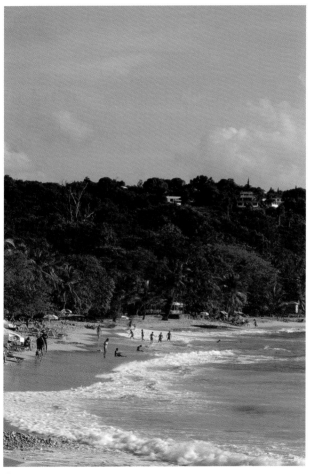

⬥ *Palm trees line the picturesque beach at Sosúa*

Puerto Plata & Playa Dorada

This Spanish settlement became notorious in 1563 when the English privateer Sir John Hawkins traded 400 slaves for pearls, hides, sugars and gold. Now the city of Puerto Plata is a thriving metropolis supported both by tourism and by the rum and tobacco industries. Those seeking out the historical richness of one of the very first European settlements of the New World will adore the Old City, and anyone looking for more excitement and bustle will enjoy the New City.

Visitors looking for package-type resort holidays flock to Playa Dorada, which is close enough to be part of the city yet is literally walled off from Puerto Plata. The region as a whole is one of the hottest spots in the country for nightlife and culture.

The Old City of Puerto Plata sits on the east side of town, beginning at the corner of Avenida Separación and Beller. Its atmosphere is elegant yet rustic, a memory of the days when it was the centre of a prosperous Victorian town. The architecture reflects both the era and the former wealth of its residents, and includes a grand, gingerbread-style mansion. A stroll along the Parque Central, located just south of the Malecón, will give you a good look at the old homes of wealthy merchants and a two-storey gazebo in Victorian style, featuring Moorish arches. There are plentiful benches and shady spots for a relaxing break or picnic.

Public buses are an inexpensive way to get from one end of town to the other and regularly bring passengers from the far end of the Malecón to the Parque Central, but they make frequent stops and can take nearly an hour and a half for one round trip. The bus is, however, still a sensible and affordable alternative for those visiting Playa Dorada on a day pass. Walking is the best option for getting around the most-visited areas of the city, since most sights are close to each other. Taxis are, as usual, a more expensive alternative, but are well worth taking for a trip that requires going any distance through the barrios or less-developed areas.

THINGS TO SEE & DO

Brugal Rum Bottling Plant

Free guided tours of the bottling process are given to visitors.
ⓐ Highway 5 (Beller 4) ⓣ 809 586 2531 ⓛ Mon–Fri 08.00–15.00

Cable car ride

This 25-minute ride to the top of Mount Isabela should not be missed.
From the top you can see the city and the coastline below.
ⓐ Circunvalación Sur on Avenida Teleférico ⓛ Mon–Sat 08.30–15.30
ⓘ Admission charge

Fuerte de San Felipe (San Felipe Fort)

One of the first forts to be built after European arrival, this grand edifice
has proven itself able to withstand even the most brutal of attacks.
It has 2.5-m (8-ft) thick walls and a deep moat, and will bring out the
adventurer in anyone. The turrets can be climbed, the old prison rooms
may be toured and there is plenty to learn in the on-site museum from
the fort's weapons collection and biographies of past residents such as
Juan Pablo Duarte.
ⓐ Avenida Colón, Puerto Plata ⓣ 809 261 6043 ⓛ 09.00–12.00,
14.00–17.00 Thur–Tues; closed Wed ⓘ Admission charge

Long Beach

Beach-goers will find the merengue loud and vibrant down on Long
Beach, which is the official beginning of Puerto Plata's Malecón. This is
a public beach, and is popular with sunbathers and party-goers. It has
also been known as a good place to spot whales during their winter
migration. Night-time on this beach does get a bit seedy, however, so
don't be surprised if you are approached by prostitutes after dark.

Malecón

Puerto Plata's Malecón is one of the hippest in the country, extending
2 km (1 mile) from Long Beach to Avenida Hermanas Mirabal. It is a

◆ *Beautiful views around Puerto Plata*

popular daytime boardwalk with shops, restaurants, and tourist vendors selling everything from fried plantains and chicken to handmade jewellery and souvenirs. The bars along the seaside strip open up in the evening (although alcoholic beverages can be bought nearly any time of day), and by sundown the beach party is in full force.

Museo del Ambar (Amber Museum)

One of the two major museums in the country dedicated to this fossilised resin, this collection is the result of three decades' dedication by the Costa family. Some of the more fantastic pieces include leaves and flowers from the Triassic and Jurassic periods, and a lizard that has been perfectly preserved for several million years. Many of the pieces of amber in the collection contain insects, plant life, water or air as old as 60 million years. The museum is spread out over two floors of the Villa Bentz mansion, a stunning architectural feat in its own right.

ⓐ Calle Duarte and Calle Castellanos ⓣ 809 586 2848 ⓛ 09.00–18.00 Mon–Sat ⓘ Admission charge

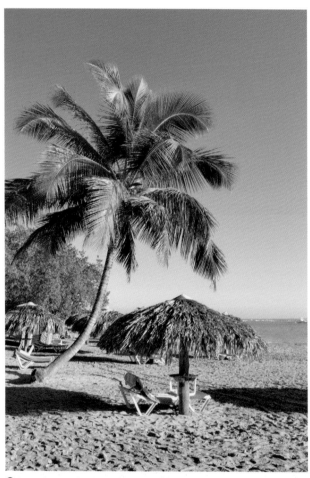

⬢ *Buy a day pass for Playa Dorada and enjoy a five-star day*

Ocean World

This immense water park enthrals both adults and children alike, combining the fun of water play with the fascination of viewing exotic animals. This park's claim to fame is the pool where you can actually swim with sharks – obviously ones that won't eat you! Another big attraction is a plexiglass window that allows you to swim past tigers in a nearby enclosure. The park also offers the chance to swim with dolphins, sea lions and many bright exotic fish. In addition, a large marina is under construction at this site.

📍 Principal 2 Cofresi 📞 809 291 1111 🔵 www.oceanworld.net 🕐 Daily
❗ Admission charge; additional charges for animal encounters

EXCURSIONS
La Isabela

Named after the Queen of Spain, this site was the second official settlement of Columbus in the New World. Recently designated a national park, this site does not have much left in the way of original structures from 1494 but has maintained its original rustic charm. Stones still map out the border of the humble church that held the first Catholic Mass of the New World, and there are other buildings that can be traced out by their foundations. A museum has been set up to display artefacts found at the site and it includes both weapons and daily items from Columbus' 1200 men, as well as many Taíno items. A cemetery is also located nearby, where the remains of a Spanish soldier have been excavated for display. To visit La Isabela, it is best to plan your trip with a tour operator within the city rather than to rent a car to make the two-and-a-half-hour drive from Puerto Plata yourself, even if it looks simple enough on a map. Road conditions in the area make the journey treacherous at best, and it is best done in professional vehicles.

Playa Dorada

If you want to hang out at the exclusive beach without buying a package at one of the 14 all-inclusives, consider getting a day pass from any one of the hotels located at Playa Dorada. The walled-in complex boasts a huge beach, golfing, tennis, dancing, and lessons for a wide variety of watersports like snorkelling and water skiing. Conveniences include several banks, a department store, a travel agency and a medical centre. Night-time at the compound is just as exciting, when three casinos light up the sky and dozens of bars, restaurants and discos keep things alive until the early morning hours.

ⓐ On Carretera 5, about 1 km (½ mile) east of Puerto Plata

TAKING A BREAK

Sam's Bar & Grill £ ❶   The hotel itself is worth a visit for its architectural grandeur. It was built in the 1890s and is proudly known as the city's first hotel. The bar specialises in Dominican food but also sells hamburgers and hot dogs. ⓐ José del Carmen Ariza 34 at Hotel Castilla ☎ 809 586 7267 ⏰ 07.00–23.00

Café Cito ££ ❷   A truly unique dining experience – you may want to play on the trampoline before you have the decadent *fillet mignon*! You can also relax and enjoy the jazz and blues, or play in the shallow pool. ⓐ Within walking distance of Playa Dorada, Sosúa highway, Km 4 ☎ 809 586 7923

Pizzeria Internacional ££ ❸   Serves expected fare and fresh seafood. ⓐ Avenida Hermanas Mirabal ☎ 809 586 4740 ⏰ Lunch and dinner

AFTER DARK

Discoteca Orión ❹   Very popular dance club, especially for merengue. ⓐ Calle 30 de Marzo 20 ☎ 809 320 8956 ⏰ 19.00–05.00

Hemingway's Bar & Grill ❺   Also serving meals, this high-end hotspot can get rowdy by early morning. ⓐ Playa Dorada Plaza ☎ 809 320 2230 ⏰ 11.00–05.00

◆ The old colonial town of Puerto Plata

Santiago

This former mining town is one of the few inland cities that still has a great nightlife and a healthy stream of visitors. It is famed as a major tobacco exporter, but more importantly as the home of the Dominican merengue. Known on the island as *merengue périco ripao*, the music for this dance is traditionally played with the *guira*, *tambora* and the accordion. There are plenty of dance clubs that are lively all night.

THINGS TO SEE & DO

Centro Cultural Eduardo León Jimenes
This is a museum of both art and anthropology, containing Taíno artefacts over 5,000 years old.
ⓐ Avenida 27 de Febrero 146 ❶ 809 582 2315 Ⓦ www.centroleon.org.do
🕔 09.00–17.00

Estadio Cibao
Santiago's professional baseball stadium is filled with enthusiasts from November to February. Baseball fans in the area during the season should always be on the lookout for their favourite stars.
ⓐ Avenida Imbert 🕔 See local newspapers for game times and ticket vendors

La Habanera Tabacalera (Cigar Factory)
The oldest cigar factory still operating in the country gives walk-through tours where aficionados can watch the entire process, beginning to end.
ⓐ Calle 16 de Agosto & Calle San Luis ❶ 809 580 4656
ⓔ info@latabacalera.com 🕔 Tours 08.30–16.30 Mon–Fri

Monumento a los Héroes de la Restauración
(Monument to the Heroes of the Restoration)
Originally built in 1940 by Rafael Trujillo in honour of himself, this impressive tower now commemorates the War of Independence from

This is essentially a full-page map image.

⬥ *Monumento a los Héroes de la Restauración offers great views of the city*

Spain. If you can make it up the stairs to the top of the 70-m (230-ft) monument, the views of the city are spectacular.

ⓐ Avenida Monumental ⓛ 09.00–12.00, 14.00–17.00 Mon–Sat

Museo Folklórico de Tomás Morel
(Tomás Morel Museum of Folk Art)

A bright and festive collection of carnival masks is the main attraction here, as well as native Taíno items and various relics from early Spanish settlers.

ⓐ Calle Restauración 174 ⓣ 809 582 6787 ⓛ 08.30–13.30, 15.30–17.30 Mon–Fri

Museo del Tabaco (Tobacco Museum)

Exhibits in this Victorian building record the history of tobacco farming and use on the island from its earliest days with the native Taíno. Visitors can learn how the crop is grown and discover how cigars are rolled.

ⓐ Calle 16 de Agosto & Calle 30 de Marzo ⓛ 09.00–12.00, 14.00–17.00 Tues–Fri, 09.00–12.00 Sat

Parque Duarte

An afternoon at the park would be incomplete without a ride in a horse-drawn carriage. Be sure to have the driver point out the 19th-century Catedral de Santiago Apóstol that sits alongside the park and is worth a visit for its stained glass and detailed mahogany carvings. This pleasant, tree-filled space is a meeting-place for locals and a good spot for watching the world go by.

TAKING A BREAK

Deli Pollo £ ❶ Fried chicken eatery with no frills. ⓐ Avenida A Guzmán 141 ⓣ 809 582 9878

Pizzeria Olé £–££ ❷ The usual fare plus Dominican-style Creole cuisine in a unique, thatched-roof setting. ⓐ Avenida J P Duarte 30 ⓣ 809 581 0410 ⓛ Daily for lunch and dinner

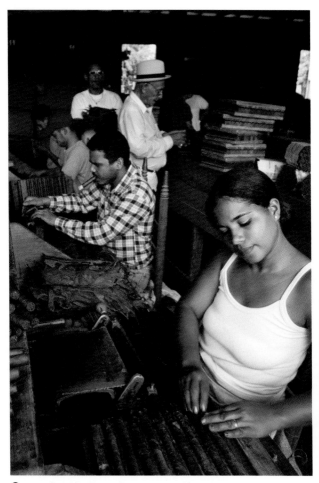

⬤ *Learn about the cigar-making process on a factory tour*

Montezuma Bar & Grill £££ ❸ Offers Dominican-style and international menu. ⓐ Prolongación Avenida Francia corner Calle Beller, in front of the Monument ❶ 809 581 1111/809 971 7130

Rancho Restaurant & Bar £££ ❹ A traditional steak house restaurant serving tasty and juicy steaks, plus fish, a few Dominican dishes and some alternatives for non-meat eaters. Its country style ambience complements the food, and there's a good selection of drinks and wines. ⓐ Avenida República de Argentina 27 ❶ 809 226 3039/3043

AFTER DARK

Alcázar ❺ Known not only for the hot merengue but also for its party-until-breakfast momentum, this is one of the best dance clubs in Santiago. Don't expect any action here until at least 01.00. ⓐ Avenida E Sadhalá 10 (at Hotel El Gran Almirante) ❶ 809 580 1992 ⓛ Nightly until 07.30

Francifol ❻ A popular nightclub in Santiago, which plays a wide range of music including rock, merengue and lounge. ⓐ Calle del Sol 125 ❶ 809 971 5558

La Vega

February brings carnival time, and with it over 50,000 tourists to this otherwise rarely visited city. Twenty city blocks are reserved for the parade, where arguably some of the very best and most elaborate masks and costumes in the nation can be seen. In fact, those looking to bring home an authentic carnival devil-mask would find the 30-km (18½-mile) ride from Santiago worthwhile for the top-quality craftsmanship and La Vega name.

La Vega Vieja, situated about 5 km (3 miles) outside La Vega, is a national historic park set up on the ruins of Columbus' 1494 settlement. His travels inland were made in attempt to find Taíno natives – unfortunately not for their cultural input, but for slavery. This was a thriving little town in its day, thanks to the discovery of gold nearby, but an earthquake levelled almost all of the buildings in 1562 and it was abandoned.

According to legend, a vision of the Virgin Mary appeared at a spot nearby, now known as **Santo Cerro** (Holy Hill). She is said to have appeared above a cross that Columbus buried in the ground during a battle with the Taíno, which gave the Spanish the upper hand to win the battle. The **Iglesia Las Mercedes** is supposed to contain relics of this cross, and is visited each year in September in pilgrimage.

TO VISIT

To reach **La Vega Vieja** or **Santo Cerro** and **La Iglesia Las Mercedes**, either take Highway 1 northeast out of La Vega, or consider hiring a taxi or touring company.
Caribe Tours ⓐ Carretera La Vega ⓣ 809 573 3488
Metro Taxi ⓐ Calle M Gómez 22 ⓣ 809 573 0303/3858
Taxi Del Cibao ⓐ Calle Manz A Multif ⓣ 809 573 0606/0200

⬭ *La Vega holds boisterous carnival celebrations*

TAKING A BREAK

Café Claro Tropical Bar £ Full bar with light lunch menu and sandwiches.
Avenida P A Rivera Km 0 809 573 9059 11.00–02.00

Express Hongri £ Inexpensive Dominican fast-food restaurant.
Avenida G Rivas 48 809 573 6953 10.00–24.00

Panaderia–Pizzeria Las Palmas £ Fresh baked breads and oven-baked
pizzas. Avenida Don M Concepción 1 809 242 0191 11.00–14.00,
17.00–22.00 Mon–Sat

Pica Pollo El Buen Sabor £ Sit-down fried chicken eatery. General J
Rodríguez 20 809 573 1097 10.00–22.00

Robert Restaurant Car Wash £ This restaurant is above the car wash
(not in it!) and food is available for take away. Autopista Duarte Km 1
809 573 0841 Daily for lunch & dinner

Mariscos Del Atlántico ££ Fresh seafood brought in daily from the coast.
Calle Restauración 51 809 242 2832 Lunch & dinner Mon–Sat

A traditional boat in the Parque Nacional del Este

Jarabacoa

Best known as a starting point for hikes up Pico Duarte, Jarabacoa is a popular mountain resort for many Dominicans. Its cooler summer climate and pine-covered scenery make a lovely backdrop for whitewater rafting, canyoning and mountain biking. The town gained its moment of fame when one of its waterfalls, Salto Jimenoa, was featured in the film *Jurassic Park*. This is also a coffee-growing region, so be sure to sample the local brew.

Although set back in the interior of the island, this small city is busy enough to have all of the modern conveniences that most tourists require. However, if you are looking for a serene mountain village, you may be disappointed by the bustle and pollution created by the numerous motorbikes and ATVs. But the Jarabacoa area is a fabulous place to experience plenty of adventure and outdoor activity.

ADVENTURE TOURS

Iguana Mama This team is a nationally recognised group of naturalists and guides that offer hiking excursions as well as the added excitement of tours, canyoning and rafting trips, and horse riding. Or alternatively you can enjoy a leisurely ride through the scenic countryside on mountain bikes.

🅐 Calle Principal 74, Cabarete 🅣 809 571 0908/0228
🅦 www.iguanamama.com

GETTING AROUND

Bear in mind that roads in this section of the country are notorious for being badly kept, and you may be well advised to let a local take you to your destination.

Taxi Jarabacoa 🅐 The taxi stand is at the corner of José Duran and Avenida Independencia, or alternatively you can call for service 🅣 809 574 7474

Bus terminal Service to La Vega 🅐 Avenida Independencia at José Duran

---

WATERFALLS

Salto Jimenoa When the water crashes from this 75-m (246-ft) fall, the mist and sun produce rainbows, making this a truly amazing sight. Take care walking along the very steep path. ⓐ The trail to the falls is off Carretera Constanza, about 7.5 km (4¼ miles) south of Jarabacoa ❶ Admission charge

Salto Jimenoa I or Lower Salto Jimenoa This waterfall is much easier to get to, but is often quite crowded, so be prepared to wait a while for a dip beneath the falls. ⓐ 3 km (almost 2 miles) east of town off Carretera Jarabacoa ❶ 08.30–19.00 ❶ Admission charge

Salto Baiguate This waterfall has an impressive cave beneath its falls, and there is also a larger swimming area for visitors. ⓐ Just south of Jarabacoa on Carretera Constanza ❶ 08.30–19.00 ❶ Admission free

Rancho Baiguate An environmentally responsible, full-service facility that offers lessons and tours for rafting, canyoning, rock wall climbing, parasailing, Pico Duarte hikes, bicycle tours of the area's waterfalls and plenty more besides. Rafting tours require a minimum age of 12, although no experience is necessary.
ⓐ Carretera La Joya 1 ❶ 809 574 6890 ⓦ www.ranchobaiguate.com

TAKING A BREAK

El Patio £ Dominican style food. ⓐ Calle M N Galán 28 ❶ 809 574 6039

Pizza & Pepperoni £ The best place to eat pizza in this town; informal atmosphere. ⓐ Gasston F Deligne 3 ❶ 809 574 4348

Pico Duarte

Pico Duarte in the Cordillera Central is the Caribbean's tallest mountain, at a height of 3,087 m (10,128 ft). The area around the mountain is largely uninhabited due to the lack of fresh water and its first recorded ascent was not until 1944, to celebrate the 100th anniversary of Dominican independence. Public trails were not even established here until the mid-1980s. However, today, around 3,000 people climb it to admire the spectacular views from the top.

Those planning a hike should be aware that the high elevation is much cooler than other parts of the island, so extra clothing and rain gear are advised. Guides are also highly recommended and are a must if you are planning on camping overnight to reach the peak. The climb itself is quite a workout, even for experienced hikers, due to the trail's uneven quality – compacted dirt gives way to loose rock and requires sturdy ankles and proper hiking boots.

Within the park and during your hike you will see many birds unique to this region, including the palm chat, which is the country's national bird. Among other birds are the red-tailed hawk, the Hispañiolan parrot and the Zumbador hummingbird. Underfoot will appear several dozen different types of amphibians. Not native to the island, wild boar roam the mountainsides along with other smaller mammals, including rodents. A wide assortment of trees includes mountain wild olive, West

HIKING ESSENTIALS

Backpack Matches or lighter fluid, food and utensils, bottled water and/or water purifier.

Rain or shine Waterproof (broken-in) hiking boots and hiking socks, waterproof sleeping bag, waterproof tent, waterproof jacket, hat and gloves, rain poncho, swimsuit.

Day pack Flashlight, first aid kit, insect repellent, sunblock, sunglasses, lip balm, toilet paper, camera and binoculars.

Indian laurel cherry, wild braziletto and Creole pine. Naturalists will also be thrilled to see the source of the Yaque del Norte River.

ADVENTURE TOURS

Iguana Mama This team's guided hikes up Pico Duarte are regarded as some of the region's best. Hikes span three days and two nights, and include dinner with a Dominican family (see page 76 for further details).

Rancho Baiguate Offers three-, four- and five-day hiking excursions to the top of Pico Duarte. The longer trip includes a hike through the Tetero Valley (see page 77 for further details).

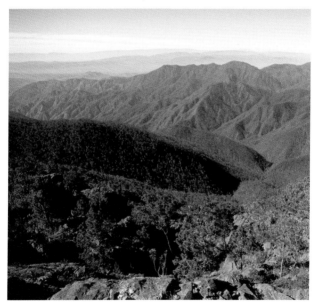

◢ *Fantastic views can be had from Pico Duarte*

Parqué Nacional los Haïtises

Located on the south coast of the Samaná Peninsula, this national park of 208 sq km (80 sq miles) is home to many historic and natural sites and is one of the most visited parks in the country. Nearly 100 plant species can be found here, including bamboo, mangrove, mahogany and cedar. Over one hundred different bird species reside in the protected area, as well as the endangered solendon, a rodent which can be found in the extensive mangrove swamps that cover the bulk of the park.

Within the park are limestone caves once used by the Taíno natives of the island, which still feature Taíno faces carved directly into the walls. The standard two-and-a-half-hour boat tour brings visitors past the major points of interest in the park, which mostly consist of the Taíno caves. One group of Taíno caves, Cueva Arena, is a popular spot to start out. Here, many boats stop and allow passengers ashore to take pictures and experience the wonder of these grottoes, with drawings depicting images of daily life and local water creatures. Other caves in the area were hideout spots for infamous pirates, which adds some excitement to the place. As the boat moves on, the San Gabriel and Remington caves are often visited for their well-known Taíno portraits – line drawings of faces on the cave walls. For bird enthusiasts, this is an opportunity to see pelicans, roseate terns, egrets and parakeets in the wild.

GETTING AROUND THE PARK

Visitors are only allowed into certain areas of the park due to its highly protected status, and these places can be visited by guided tour only. You can visit the park on foot but there are not many trails cut through and its swampy terrain makes it difficult to pass at best – the easiest way to get around is by boat. Many of the caves that you would want to view are located on the coast, and tours will bring you directly into the swamps, where you will be able to see the wildlife and the amazing drawings up close.

There are two ways to tour the park by boat. You can take a ferry from Samaná (the landing is located on the Malecón across from the

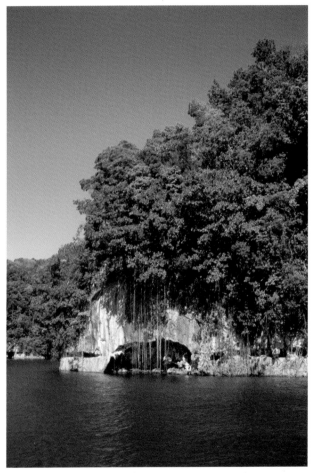

⬥ The Parqué Nacional los Haïtises is a great place to explore

Banco Popular) to the town of Sabana de la Mar, where there is a choice of any number of *buscones* who will approach tourists for a group of two to four to ride out on a small boat for a one- to two-and-a-half-hour tour of the coast. Expect to pay extra for a guide to explain what you are seeing, and save a small amount for your park entrance fee.

The alternative is to book an excursion with a tour operator in Samaná, where you can often get a package that includes a round-trip fare, guide and lunch.

BOAT TOUR OPERATORS

Moto Marina Departing directly from Samaná, this excursion operator begins the tour in true Dominican style with a rum cocktail. Within half an hour, you are in the park and enjoying all it has to offer, with a fully trained guide. Snacks and lunch are served on the beach at the Taíno caves, and guests have the option of stopping by Cayo Levantado for swimming before going back to home port.
ⓐ Avenida Malecón ⓣ 809 538 2302 ⓔ motomarina@yahoo.com

MS Tours SA Offering full-service, round-trip tours with guides directly from Samaná.
ⓐ Avenida Malecón 7 ⓣ 809 538 2499/3343 ⓔ ms_tours@hotmail.com

Victoria Marine Two departure points are offered with this tour, which includes guide, transportation and lunch.
ⓐ Malecón ⓣ 809 538 2494 ⓛ Two tours daily, departing 09.00 & 13.30
ⓐ Cayo Levantado ⓣ 809 538 2494 ⓛ Two tours daily, departing 09.30 & 14.00

Parque Nacional del Este & Isla Saona

This national park, located in the extreme south-east of the country, contains some of the most extraordinary wildlife and historical sites on the island, and includes Isla Saona, a beautiful island off the southern coast. The park itself is suited for hiking and boating, and is not accessible to tourists in vehicles. These coastal regions are a magnificent place to see several endangered species, including the West Indian manatee, sea turtles and bottlenose dolphins, as well as rhinoceros, iguana and hutia. The park is also home to several Taíno sites of historical importance.

A birdwatcher's paradise, this densely forested area is home to 112 known species. Several of these are unique to the island, such as the white-headed dove and the Hispañiolan lizard cuckoo. Offshore, surrounding waters are a good place to look for migrating humpback whales during January and February, and to view the West Indian

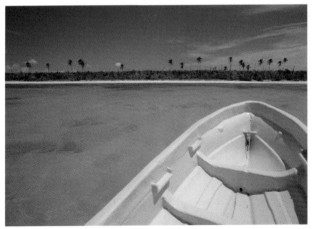

🔺 *Parque Nacional del Este is a haven for many endangered species*

manatee, a large, grey aquatic mammal also known as a sea cow; its nearest land relative is the elephant.

ISLA SAONA

Visitors to this small island will find it populated with plenty of birds, but beware – there are nearly as many tacky tourist joints. This once-pristine island, although technically protected by national park status, has fallen victim to over-use, knocking the marine ecosystem out of balance due in part to over-fishing and illegal hunting, which has contributed to the extinction of vertebrates such as the Caribbean monk seal. The Nature Conservancy is now working with the Dominican Republic in an effort to re-establish this balance and save the fragile coral reefs that have been partially destroyed by just a couple of decades of careless snorkelling. It is still a beautiful place to visit, however, with some of the most picturesque beaches and palm forests imaginable.

Caves within the park are the main sites containing artefacts from Taíno times, primarily **Cueva José María**, **Cueva del Puente**, and a more obscure site near **Peñon Gordo** which requires a guide. The most fascinating objects are petroglyphs and pictographs depicting some of the first encounters between the native tribes and the Spanish invaders. All of these areas require a great deal of hiking – be well equipped with insect repellent, sunscreen and a good amount of fresh water.

It is easiest to visit the park on an organised tour. However, if not, you must pay the entrance fee at the national park office (ⓐ Playa Bayahibe ⓣ 809 833 0022 ⓛ 08.30–12.30) and hire a park ranger as a guide, which is an additional charge. Some hire a private boat to motor around the coastal waters of the park, but if you plan on setting foot on park territory, you must have a guide.

TOUR OPERATORS FOR THE PARK

Casa Daniel Includes passage and lunch with guide. ⓐ Calle Principe 1, Playa Bayahibe ⓣ 809 833 0050

ScubaFun Boat tour with meal included. ⓐ Calle Principe 28, Playa Bayahibe ⓣ 809 833 0003

Lago Enriquillo & Isla Cabritos

Sitting between Sierra de Neiba to the north and Sierra Barohuco to the south is the valley that is home to Lago Enriquillo and the Parque Nacional Isla Cabritos. This area has been a national park for decades, protecting not only the lowest point in the Caribbean – 44 m (144 ft) below sea level – but also many endangered species and several places of historic interest. The park consists of the island it is named after as well as Lago Enriquillo and its surrounding shores.

Lago Enriquillo was at one time a channel that connected Port-au-Prince and the Bahía de Neiba, which was stranded inland when the earth's continental plates shifted. The result was a saltwater lake, which is constantly fed by rivers flowing from the surrounding mountains. It sits only 42 km (26 miles) from the border of Haiti.

Having once been completely under water, the shores of the lake still contain pieces of coral from prehistoric times. Living in the rivers that feed the lake is an abundance of American crocodiles, most readily found in the Río de La Descubierta and avoiding the salt water. This river is a favourite place for flamingos to flock, and you will probably be able to spot a heron here.

The lake was named after the Taíno chief Enriquillo, who resisted the Spaniards for nearly 15 years by hiding out in the surrounding caves. He and his followers held out long enough to eventually achieve a peace treaty with the Spaniards, but unfortunately Enriquillo died of smallpox soon afterward. He is commemorated by a statue along Route 46.

ISLA CABRITOS

The Parque Nacional Isla Cabritos is on the largest of three islands found in the centre of Lake Enriquillo, the other two being the smaller and rarely visited islands of Barbarita and Islita. Isla Cabritos, which translates as 'Little Goats' Island', sits 4–40 m (13–130 ft) below sea level in Lago Enriquillo, and was at one time completely under water. It is 12 km (7½ miles) long and is mostly a flat, desert habitat. It receives less than 50 cm (20 in) of rainfall each year and temperatures sometimes climb to 44°C (112°F). The landscape is peppered with cacti and is home to an astounding number of reptiles, including the endangered rhinoceros iguana and Ricord iguana. Many of the iguanas on the island are over 20 years old and as large and tame as housecats, accustomed to the frequent visitors that often stop by with less-than-healthy snacks. The island is also home to a number of birds, including the West Indian nighthawk and the burrowing owl.

Those interested in Taíno art will want to visit Las Caritas ('the little faces'), which is located near the park entrance on the highway. If you are up for a rocky climb, you can get up close to these petroglyphs that are visible from the road below, which are actually carved into petrified coral, not rock. Many believe that these mark a special ceremonial site, although little is known about them.

TOURS IN THE PARK

Tours are conducted by boat and can last from one to two-and-a-half hours, so bring plenty of fresh water and sunscreen. Isla Cabritos is less intense, and is good for viewing large iguanas, which are friendly to tourists. Morning tours are the best for viewing wildlife, especially crocodiles, and the most comfortable for passengers. Guides are not usually very talkative nor informative, but the scenery should be sufficient to keep you well occupied. Most tours stop on the island for a walk about. Visitor information is available from the Division of National Parks (📍 Calle Damas 6, Old City, Santo Domingo ☎ 809 685 1316).

> The entrance to Lago Enriquillo and Isla Cabritos park area is marked by a bright yellow and green sign, 3 km (almost 2 miles) east of La Descubierta along Highway 46. 🕐 07.00–17.00 ❶ Admission charge

Discovering amber

Amber is one of the Dominican Republic's best-known products, and if you admire this unusual gemstone, it can provide the theme for several interesting places to visit, from jewellery shops, galleries and museums to a hiking excursion and to the mines themselves.

Unlike most gemstones, which are mineral in origin, amber is formed when resin that has seeped out of trees is fossilised. What makes amber even more fascinating is that prehistoric insects, plants, spiders, feathers and even the occasional lizard or frog can be found trapped inside it. Don't expect to find any examples of the latter for sale, however – they are very rare.

Dominican amber is especially clear and has a higher incidence of trapped insects, making it some of the most sought-after in the world. Although most amber is in shades of yellow and brown, it is sometimes found in red, rarely in a dusty green colour and – only in the Dominican Republic – in blue. Dominican amber is about 25 million years old, and the insects and plants it contains have been extinct for many millions of years – so has the species of tree that formed the resin.

Most of the Dominican Republic's amber comes from two areas; in the mountains north of the city of Santiago and around the towns of El Valle and Cotui, north-east of Santo Domingo. A small amount comes from the Bayaguana area, in the east near Sabana, but it is younger – a mere 15–17 million years old.

The best quality – the oldest and the hardest – is that from the La Cumbre region, in the central Cordillera Septentrional mountain range between Puerto Plata and Santiago. The La Toca, Palo Quemado, La Bucara, and Los Cacaos mines are in this region, revealing amber that is 33–40 million years old. Slightly younger – about 25 million years old – is the amber found in the Palo Alto area, also near Santiago. The Los Cacaos mines are the source of the very rare blue amber.

⬤ *Amber mining and jewellery making are important industries*

THINGS TO SEE & DO

Galería de Ambar
Although it includes more Dominican products than amber and has a strong shopping component, Galería de Ambar does have interesting exhibits, as well as signage in English.

ⓐ Calle 12 de Julio, Puerto Plata ☎ 809 586 6467
ⓦ www.ambercollection.itgo.com 🕐 08.30–18.00 Mon–Fri, 09.00–13.00 Sat

FAKE OR REAL?
To the untrained eye, a fly or a bit of dried flower that was encased in orange-coloured plastic a week ago can look very convincingly like a piece of amber millions of years old. To complicate matters, copal – unfossilised resin of a much younger age – can also contain insects and plants, and has a similar colour. How can you be sure what you're getting is real amber? Here are some tips from the experts:

Know the source If you shop at a museum shop or a well-known and reputable jeweller, you can be sure of getting the real thing – and in top quality.

Rub the stone vigorously The ancient Greek name for amber – *electron* – is the basis for our word electricity. The Greeks first noticed that if you rub amber repeatedly on a piece of cotton cloth, it will generate static electricity that will attract hair or other light natural substance. Neither plastic nor copal will do this.

Look at it under fluorescent light If the stone glows with a changed colour, it is real. Reputable dealers will have fluorescent lamps available so that you can perform this simple test and confirm that you are spending money on the real thing.

Amber Museum

The island's best and most complete amber museum is the life work of a Dominican family, located in this gracious old mansion. The collections, begun in 1970, are not only varied, but contain some of the world's rarest examples of amber – including an amber-encased lizard – one of fewer than two dozen ever found. Flowers, insects and mosses are also to be found, preserved as if yesterday, inside the specimens.

ⓐ Villa Bentz, Calle Duarte and Castellanos, Puerto Plata ⓣ 809 586 2848
ⓦ www.ambermuseum.com ⓛ Mon–Sat 09.00–18.00, closed Sun
ⓘ Admission charge

Museo de Historia Natural (Natural History Museum)

Geology forms a major part of this museum, which helps put amber into the larger picture of the island's formation. Learn how fossils were formed, as well as the natural history of amber. If you have children with you, there is plenty to keep them occupied while you learn about amber.

ⓐ Plaza de la Cultura, Santo Domingo ⓣ 809 689 0106 ⓛ 10.00–17.00, closed Mon ⓘ Admission charge

Museo Mundo de Ambar (Amber World Museum)

This museum's informative displays of Dominican amber include examples in several colours, as well as a wide variety of flora and fauna embedded in the stones. In the workshop you can see raw amber being polished and set into jewellery, which you can buy in the museum shop.

ⓐ Arz. Merino 452 (Zona Colonial), Santo Domingo ⓣ 809 686 5700
ⓦ www.amberworldmuseum.com ⓛ 09.00–18.00

Visiting amber mines

The most easily visited amber mines are those in the mountains between Puerto Plata and Santiago. The mines are near the crest of the mountains, where the amber lies between layers of sandstone that has been uplifted. Often these veins are discovered when a landslide exposes a strata of black lignite among the lighter sandstone. This is where the pieces of amber will be found. Depending on the angle of these layers,

DISCOVERING AMBER

pits are dug into the mountain or into the cliffs. The amber is painstakingly carved out by hand, with chisels and machetes.

It is important to arrive at the mines with a realistic view of what to expect. For example, hoping to see any semblance of elaborate mining operations will prove disappointing. The sites are scattered and usually consist of a hole or shaft, roughly supported by a few logs. Workmen burn candles – this warns them of decreased oxygen in the air – and the only 'building' is likely to be a shelter of tarpaulin on sticks.

Although no regularly scheduled tours go to the mines from the resorts, it is possible to arrange one if you ask around, especially at the **Amber Museum** in Puerto Plata (see page 90). Or contact **Tours Trips Treks & Travel** (🕿 809 867 8884 🕿 206 600 1700 🌐 www.4Tdomrep.com).

SHOPPING FOR AMBER

Raw amber is usually polished to bring out its lustre and to show off the insects or plant life encased in it. Some of the shops have craftsmen working there, so you can see this process. Another unusual gem called larimar, a semi-precious turquoise blue stone found only in the Dominican Republic, is often sold in the same shops as amber.

Ambar Tres 🏠 La Atarazana 3, Zona Colonial, Santo Domingo 🕿 809 688 0474

The Amber Factory 🏠 Arz. Merino 452, Zona Colonial, Santo Domingo 🕿 809 686 5700 🌐 www.amberfactory.com

Amber Shop 🏠 Playa Dorada Plaza, Puerto Plata 🕿 809 209 2215 🕑 09.00–18.00, closed Sun

Museo de Ambar Dominicano Gift Shop 🏠 Duarte 61, Puerto Plata 🕿 809 586 2848 🕑 09.00–18.00, closed Sun

Museo Larimar Dominicano 🏠 Isabela la Católica, Santo Domingo 🕿 809 689 6605 🕑 09.00–18.00

Patrick's Silversmithy 🏠 Pedro Clisante 9, Sosúa 🕿 809 571 2121

Diving excursions

For many underwater lovers, diving is what the Dominican Republic is all about. The extraordinary reefs and waters surrounding its beautiful beaches are filled with colourful sea life, and diving services offer equipment and lessons. A wide array of fish species from nurse sharks to green moray eels can be seen on your underwater travels.

EAST OF SANTO DOMINGO

Parque Nacional Submarino La Caleta, about 35 km (22 miles) east of the capital, is a coral-reef in process around the scuttled treasure hunt ship *The Hickory*. Reaching to 180 m (590 ft), the protected area is perfect for divers who want to explore the open hull and the tropical sea life that frequents it. There is no official diving service setup, so make arrangements with your resort or with a diving service nearby.

Scuba Caribe SA This outfit offers diving services in five different locations in Punta Cana , with lessons and rentals for beginners through to experienced scuba divers.
ⓐ Carretera Friusa 1 ⓣ 809 221 1336/809 552 0379

SAMANÁ PENINSULA

The best dive sites in this area are Dive The Tower, a mountain rising from the sea, with a 50-m (165-ft) submerged mountainside alive with brilliant sea life, and **La Catedral**, a huge, underwater cave that has formed an air pocket. For advanced divers, **Plaza Monica** is a reef 30 m (100 ft) down, with a large population of sea life. At **Cabo Cabron**, divers may even hear the songs of migrating whales.

Dive Samaná A company that provides rentals and transportation to diving locations in the area.
ⓐ Casa Marina Bay Resort ⓣ 809 538 0020 ⓦ www.amhsamarina.com
ⓛ Daily

Stellina Dive Centre This place makes dive trips by advance reservation to both the popular and little-known sites.
ⓐ Hotel Cacao Beach, Las Terrenas ☎ 809 240 6000

AMBER COAST

The dive capital of this north coast is **Sosúa**, where there are dozens of sites, for all skill levels. Reefs swim with spectacular fish, and are easy to reach. Most of these are multi-faceted reefs, with plenty of opportunities for beginners but enough depth to satisfy experts as well.

The sunken cargo ship *Zingara* lies 36 m (118 ft) below the surface, with a shallow reef wall above where novice divers can enjoy the fan corals and tube sponges. Experienced divers should aim for **Paradise Reef**, which also has something for everyone, with a bright coral reef at about 12 m (39 ft), and octopus and squid at 32 m (105 ft). **Garden of Los Charamicos** has large sponges and bright fan corals at a maximum depth of 24 m (79 ft). **Pyramids** was formed by erosion, with corals at

⬥ *A diver exploring the coral reef at Punta Cana*

15 m (49 ft) down. One of the best spots is **Airport Wall**, a 24 m (79 ft) area with several caves and some elkhorn coral.

Gri-Gri Divers A wide variety of packages for all levels is available here, and trips are offered to 13 different nearby dive sites. The fully certified staff is multilingual.
ⓐ Río San Juan ☎ 809 589 2671

Hippocampo Dive Centre This centre has individual and group diving classes for beginners and brush-up courses for those who have not dived recently. A good selection of rentals and equipment for sale makes this a full-service dive shop.
ⓐ Carretera Cabarete ☎ 809 571 0834

Soficap This company offers diving equipment rentals and instruction for the Cabarete beach area.
ⓐ Carretera Cabarete ☎ 809 571 0280 ◷ Daily, by appointment

SAFETY FIRST
Most resorts offer diving services or can put you in touch with a reliable guide. This is much safer than making independent plans with the local fishermen, since the professional dive boats are equipped with proper safety devices and are operated by trained divers.

◗ *Take pleasure in the island's artwork*

LIFESTYLE

Food & drink

The traditional foods of the Dominican people are a mixture of ancient recipes from Taíno tribes and the influences of Spanish settlers and other European and African populations. Beans and rice are the staple food and chicken is the most popular meat, often found fried or roasted at informal eateries along the streets and beaches. Rum is by far the most well-known Dominican drink, but locals enjoy plenty of non-alcoholic fruit drinks as well, taking full advantage of their tropical treats.

SPECIALITIES
Casabe
Made from the yucca (also known as cassava), a large tuber native to the island of Hispañiola, this dish is made in almost exactly the same way it was back in Taíno times. The plant is hand-ground, pressed and flattened into discs and then baked into a tortilla-like sheet. These are very high in fibre and low in fat, and are eaten with meals or alone as a snack.

Pan de agua
A medium-length bread translated as, simply, 'water bread', it contains yeast and is another staple in the Dominican diet.

DESSERTS
Harina de maíz (corn meal pudding)
Also served as a breakfast dish, this dish is prepared with evaporated milk and is a sweetened version of polenta, with cinnamon and nutmeg added. It can be served warm or cold.

Masitas (coconut biscuits)
A simple cookie made from fresh coconut chunks, found throughout the country.

Flan (caramel cream pudding)

Originally brought to the island by the Spanish, this thick, corn-based dessert made with egg yolks and heavy cream is a particular favourite of Dominicans.

Jalea de batata (sweet potato pudding)

A very sweet delicacy prepared with shredded coconut, milk, butter, cloves, cinnamon and sweet potato.

MEAL TIMES
Breakfast

If you have a sensitive stomach, plan to stay in for the continental spread at your hotel – Dominican breakfasts are traditionally hearty and rich, designed for farmworkers preparing for a long day in the fields. It is not unusual to see a local restaurant serving deep-fried salami and cheese to accompany fried eggs and onions with ham. To expand on the food groups, there may be a few slices of boiled yucca, and certainly a freshly roasted and brewed cup of sweet coffee with milk.

Dinner (lunch)

Served during the time that most western countries refer to as lunch, this large meal precedes siesta. Lasting an average of at least an hour and possibly more, it features a hearty meat course with a vegetable such as green beans, as well as a starch such as sweet potato or rice. Favourite meat dishes include *rabo encendido*, which is a spicy soup made from oxtails, or *asopao*, a general name for a rice-based soup that may have seafood, chicken, pork or beef and an assortment of spices.

Supper

The final meal of the day, supper is often served late in the evening after the air has cooled and the family has had a chance to return home. Traditionally it is the meal when the family gets together, and the focus is less on eating and more on socialising. Typical dishes at the late meal are chicken based, such as *pica pollo*, which is breaded fried chicken.

○ *Dominican rum is used to create many exotic cocktails*

FRUITS

Here you can find many of the exotic fruits that are rare and expensive at home, so fill up on guava smoothies, chilled passionfruit, or the Dominican favourite, *morir soñando*, which includes fresh orange juice, sugar and milk blended together. Bananas and star fruit are just a few of the other options for a fresh drink or fruit salad, and everyone should try fresh coconut milk before leaving the island.

BEVERAGES
Rum
Of the Dominican rums, Bermúdez is considered the best. The quality to look for in buying your rum is its colour (the darker, the better) and its age. Barceló and Brugal brands are also considered top quality, but there are many private labels that your concierge or a local merchant may recommend that should not be overlooked. If you want your rum to last the evening, order a *cuba libre servicio* and you will get a bottle of rum, two cokes and a bucket of ice. Check that the ice was not frozen from the local tap water before you drink, though.

Mabi
Mabi has a rather low alcohol content compared to rum, and is made with the native plant, *behuco de indio*. The processed vine is mixed with brown sugar and water and fermented in the sun for three days, resulting in a cider-like drink.

Beer & wine
There are plenty of beers to choose between. Most popular is the island's Presidente, which comes in a bottle that might be much larger than you are used to, so be sure to work up a thirst before ordering.

Dominican wines are perhaps worth a sip for the experience, but do not go searching too far – the country is not well known for its fine national vintages and imported wines are expensive. If you are looking for a genuine wine drink of the locals, seek out *mama juana*, a concoction of wine, rum, honey and plants, which is fermented both underground and in the sun to create supposed aphrodisiac qualities.

Non-alcoholic beverages
In addition to a plethora of fruit juices that can be served alone mixed or blended with ice, the Dominican Republic is well known as a coffee producer. In fact, some of the finest coffees in the world are grown and roasted here; locals enjoy it as an after-meal beverage with sugar and with or without milk.

Menu decoder

MEALS & BEVERAGES

Asopao Thick soup made with rice and seafood or meat

Bandera dominicana Typical Dominican lunch of rice, beans and meat

Casabe Cassava bread, thick tortilla made with dried yucca

Chicharrón Fried pork rind

Cocido Meaty stew

Fría A very cold beer (literally means 'cold')

Locrio A combination of rice, meat (maybe seafood) and vegetables

Longaniza Spicy pork sausage

Mabi Cider-like alcoholic beverage

Mangú Mashed plantains, yucca, and yautía

Moro Traditional dish made with rice and beans

Pica pollo Breaded fried chicken

Puerco en puya Pork roasted on a spit

Rabo encendido Spicy oxtail soup

Res guisada Beef stew

Sancocho A Dominican stew made with up to seven types of meat

COMMON TERMS

Al ajillo In garlic sauce

Al horno Food cooked in the oven

Al oregano With double cream and oregano sauce

Con coco With coconut milk, tomato, and garlic sauce

Criolla With spicy, tomato-based sauce

Mariscos Seafood

Picadera Buffet or appetisers

Picante Spicy hot

Pincho Brochette/kebab

Salsa de tomate Tomato paste

COMMON INGREDIENTS

Aguacate Avocado

Arroz Rice

Auyama Gem squash (also known as calabaza)

Bacalao Codfish
Batata Sweet potato (also known as camote and boniato)
Bija anato, annato or **achiote** Red seeds used to color foods
China Orange
Chivo Goat
Cilantro Coriander
Garbanzos Chick peas
Guayaba Guava
Guineo Banana
Habas Broad beans
Habichuelas pintas Kidney beans
Lambí Conch
Langosta Clawless lobster
Leche Milk
Lechoza pawpaw Usually known as papaya (or simply pawpaw)

Limoncillo Spanish lemon
Maní Peanuts (also known as cacahuate or cacahuete)

Mondongo Tripe (also known as panza, tripas or menudos)
Naranja Orange
Nuez moscada Nutmeg
Papa Potato
Plátano Plantain
Pulpo Octopus
Remolacha Beet
Salsa inglesa Worcestershire sauce
Vainitas Green beans
Yucca Cassava, root of the yucca plant, also known as mandioca

LIFESTYLE

Shopping

There are a couple of important things to remember when shopping in the Dominican Republic. Firstly, pickpockets target tourists, so conceal your money and important papers well, and do not carry large amounts of money on you or take out large sums from ATMs. Secondly, haggling for your price is expected in most settings.

MARKETS
To find authentic local markets, which are usually held every day in large cities and less frequently in smaller towns, it is best to ask your host or any local to point you in the right direction.

AMBER & LARIMAR
Museo Larimar Dominicano ⓐ Isabela la Católica, Santo Domingo
ⓣ 809 689 6605 ⓛ 09.00–18.00

Museo del Ambar Dominicano Gift Shop ⓐ Duarte 61, Puerto Plata
ⓣ 809 586 3910 ⓛ 09.00–18.00 Mon–Sat, closed Sun

CIGARS & TOBACCO
Cigar King ⓐ El Conde 458, Santo Domingo ⓣ 809 685 0278
ⓛ 09.30–12.00 & 15.00–17.30 Mon–Sat, closed Sun

Cuevas y Hermanos Fabricantes de Cigarros ⓐ Avenida General López,
Puerto Plata ⓣ 809 970 0903 ⓛ 13.00–17.00 & 21.00–24.00 Tues–Sun,
closed Mon

MAJOR SHOPPING CITIES
Santiago (see page 66) The city's main shopping district is Calle del Sol.

La Romana (see page 32) Altos de Chavón is an upmarket shopping complex with a wide range of shops, and there are also plenty of very good restaurants.

🔺 *Colourful local artwork for sale*

Santo Domingo (see page 14) Try El Mercado Modelo for authentic native crafts (ⓐ Calle Mella, Zona Colonial). Calle El Conde is a reasonably priced shopping district with trendy shops (ⓐ Zona Colonial), and if you want international brand-name boutiques head for Plaza Central (ⓐ Avenida Winston Churchill and Avenida 27 de Febrero) or Acropolis (ⓐ Avenida Winston Churchill).

Sosúa (see page 53) Visit Taimascaros to see an astonishing collection of carnival art including masks and costumes (ⓐ Camino Libre 70 ⓕ 809 571 3138).

Puerto Plata (see page 59) Has a large souvenir market, called Mercado Nuevo, that is renowned for good, old-fashioned haggling (ⓐ Off El Morro between Villa Nueva and Avenida José Ramón López).

Children

Dominicans love children and they are welcome in all but the most expensive restaurants, expecially in the resort towns. The resorts have plenty of activities on offer and often have good childcare facilities too.

FUN ATTRACTIONS & WATER PARKS

Agua Splash

A typical water park with waterslides and pools (see page 16).

ⓐ Avenida España 50, Santo Domingo ❶ 809 766 1927 ◕ 11.00–19.00 Tues–Sun

Columbus Aquaparque

Equipped with shops, restaurants, and bars to keep the landlubbers content (see page 55).

ⓐ Carretera Sosúa Plata, Sosúa ❶ 809 571 2642/2254 ◕ 10.00–18.00

FunCity Action Park

Go-carts, bumper cars, grand prix and more, plus a special kiddie section for ages 2–8, with food and beverages on site (see page 55).

ⓐ Carretera Puerto Plata, Km 5, Sosúa ❶ 809 320 1031

ⓦ www.funcity-gocarts.com ◕ Daily ❶ Admission charge; shuttle services to and from Sosúa and other nearby towns

Parque Zoológico Nacional (National Zoo)

Kids will love the crocodiles, hyenas and other wild beasts here (see page 17).

ⓐ Avenida La Vega Real, Arroyo Hondo, Santo Domingo ❶ 809 562 3149 ◕ Daily 09.00–17.00 ❶ Admission charge

Rancho Cumayasa Eco

This resort is home to the popular children's attraction 'Hurricane House' (see page 34).

ⓐ Highway 4, La Romana ❶ 809 556 1606 ❶ Non-guests need to buy a day pass, which includes lunch, a one-hour horse ride, and access to the paddleboats and other facilities.

Ocean World

Swimming with sharks, dolphins, sea lions and more (see page 63).
ⓐ Principal 2 Cofresí, Puerto Plata ❶ 809 291 1111 Ⓦ www.oceanworld.net
🕒 Daily

WHALE WATCHING

Whale Samaná & Victoria Marine, Samaná (❶ 809 538 2494)
Two departure points are offered (Jan–Mar):
Malecón 🕒 Two tours daily 09.00 & 13.30
Cayo Levantado 🕒 Two tours daily 09.30 & 14.00

Moto Marina Whale watching tours. ⓐ Avenida Malecón 3, Samaná
❶ 809 538 2302 ⓔ motomarina@yahoo.com 🕒 Jan–Mar

🔺 *Swimming with dolphins at Ocean World*

Sports & activities

BASEBALL

No other sport takes hold of the Dominican Republic like *béisbol*; it is an unofficial national religion. Currently there are over 400 Dominican players in the US Major Leagues (for more details on Dominican players, see ⓦ www.baseball-reference.com). The season runs October–January but is played year-round by kids in the streets or adults in the country's various stadiums. Tickets are usually sold-out well in advance, but there are always 'scalpers' or touts selling tickets outside the stadiums. Check also with your hotel concierge or taxi driver as you never know what connections they might have and it could be much cheaper for you.

Baseball Stadiums
Estadio Quisqueya (Quisqueya Stadium) ⓐ Avenida Tiradentes, Santo Domingo ⓣ 809 540 5772 ⓛ Game times vary ⓘ Admission charge
Estadio Tetelo Vargas (Tetelo Vargas Stadium) ⓐ Avenida Circunvalación & Carretera Mella ⓘ Admission charge
Online baseball and event tickets ⓦ www.ticketexpress.com

COCKFIGHTING

This tradition is a highly controversial, but deeply ingrained part of Dominican culture. Weekends are cockfighting days in almost every town and city in the country. These events are accompanied by an almost carnivalesque atmosphere of drinking, betting and yelling.
ⓐ In Santo Domingo, fights take place at the Coliseo Galístico de Santo Domingo on Avenida Luperón

GOLF

Most golf courses are to be found along the coast in the country's burgeoning resorts. The three best are at Casa de Campo in La Romana, Playa Dorada and Playa Grande. The latter two are the most reasonable, but green fees at the Teeth of the Dog course at Casa de Campo will cost you a hefty sum.

WATERSPORTS

Water lovers will find no shortage of activities on offer at any of the resorts on the island. Try your hand at windsurfing, snorkelling, parasailing, sailing, deep sea fishing and more. Cabarete (see page 46) is considered one of the finest windsurfing locations in the world and scuba diving and kiteboarding are also on offer. Whether you're an experienced diver or a beginner, exploring the spectacular array of colourful marine life and shipwrecks in the incredibly clear Caribbean waters is a must. See 'Diving excursions' on page 92 for more details. For snorkelling, the beach at La Isabela on the north coast, though best known for its Columbus connection (see page 63), also boasts an incredible array of underwater life.

◆ *Explore the waters by sailing boat*

LIFESTYLE

Festivals & events

CARNIVAL

Celebrated every Sunday in February and ending in a huge event at the end of the month right before Lent, Carnival is an exciting time all over the island. The cities of La Vega, Santiago, Monte Cristi and Santo Domingo hold the most boisterous and well known celebrations nationwide, drawing in crowds from all over the world. Residents spend the entire year working on their costumes, which are often a work of art. Masks depicting *el Diablo* (the devil) are very common, as well as bright and festive dresses. If you are planning on watching a parade, beware of the more violent traditions, including flailing whips and heavy balloons.

MERENGUE FESTIVAL

In July and August each year, Santo Domingo is host to an enormous merengue festival where the best of the best dancers perform all over the city. It is hard to miss the excitement, even if you try!

Early October is Puerto Plata's annual merengue festival, located on its Malecón (promenade). For the festivities, the area is converted into a fairgrounds of sorts, with only foot traffic allowed and local crafts and foods for sale.

LATIN MUSIC FESTIVAL

Held at the Olympic Stadium in Santo Domingo every two years in September, the Latin Music Festival attracts internationally known Latin musicians who showcase and celebrate the art form, spanning the genres of salsa, merengue, bachata and jazz.

CREOLE MUSIC FESTIVAL

This festival, held the last weekend in October each year, is the newest festival on the island, having run for only the past nine years or so. It features some of the most renowned musical groups and soloists from the Creole-speaking world. Musical forms include calypso, soukous and zydeco (from the US state of Louisiana).

Participants wear flamboyant costumes for the Santo Domingo Carnival

NATIONAL & CULTURAL HOLIDAYS AT A GLANCE

1 January	New Year's Day
6 January	Three Kings' Day/Epiphany
21 January	Our Lady of Altagracia
26 January	Duarte Day
27 February	Independence Day
March/April (Easter Week)	Semana Santa
14 April	Pan American Day
1 May	Labour Day
10 June	Feast of Corpus Christi
16 July	Foundation of Sociedad la Trinitaria
16 August	Restoration Day
24 September	Our Lady of Mercedes
12 October	Columbus Day
24 October	UN Day
1 November	All Saints' Day
6 November	Constitution Day
25 December	Christmas Day

TRAVELLING DURING NATIONAL HOLIDAYS

You may find that banks, government offices, museums and some shops are closed on these days. There are also often parades and other festivities that may block off roads or several city blocks and deter plans on the short term. It is always wise to ask your host for advice before travelling on your own during these times. **Semana Santa**, Easter Week, is the time during which you will most likely be inconvenienced by the holiday status. Strangely enough, although watersports are prohibited during this time, this is when you will find beaches and pools at their most crowded, as well as hotels and just about everywhere else.

▶ *Getting about in the Dominican Republic*

Accommodation

The following is a brief selection of hotels per areas, graded by approximate price, based on a double room per night.

£ = under $100   ££ = $100–$180   £££ = $180–$260

SANTO DOMINGO

Aparthotel Delta ££ A small, friendly hotel in central Santo Domingo.
ⓐ Avenida Sarasota 53, Bella Vista ❶ 809 535 0800
Ⓦ www.hoteldelta.com.do

Hotel Santo Domingo ££–£££ Set in lush tropical gardens, but centrally located, this hotel is popular with international business travellers.
ⓐ Avenida Independencia ❶ 809 221 1511
Ⓦ www.hotelsantodomingo.com.do

BOCA CHICA

Oasis Hamaca £££ The biggest hotel in the Boca Chica area, convenient both for the beach at Boca Chica and for the city of Santo Domingo.
❶ 809 523 4611 Ⓦ www.coralhamaca.com

SAN PEDRO DE MACORIS

Coral Costa Caribe ££ A modern hotel set in secluded grounds.
ⓐ Juan Dolio ❶ 809 526 2244 Ⓦ www.coralcostacaribe.com

Hotel Santana Beach Resort & Casino £££ Enjoy the excellent sports facilities and luxuries, then watch the sunset from the beach.
ⓐ Carretera Romana, San Pedro de Macoris, km 14 ❶ 809 412 1010
Ⓦ www.santanabeach.com

LA ROMANA

Casa de Campo Hotel ££–£££ The exclusive resort, famous for its celebrated golf courses and shopping phenomenon at Altos de Chavón.
ⓐ La Romana ❶ 809 523 3333 Ⓦ www.casadecampo.com.do

PUNTA CANA

Natura Park ££ This idyllic low-rise resort set in a large garden is built using local natural resources in an ecologically friendly style. It offers a host of facilities and activities. ⓐ Cabeza de Toro, Punta Cana ⓣ 809 221 2626 ⓦ www.blau-hotels.com

SAMANÁ

Gran Bahia Principe El Portillo £££ Built on a calm stretch of coast, the abundant coral reef means the snorkeling is great. ⓐ El Portillo Beach, Las Terrenas, Samaná ⓣ 809 240 6100 ⓦ www.bahia-principe.com

CABARETE

Aparthotel Caracol Cabarete ££ Located on the beach, this hotel is aimed at independent travellers and families wanting to make the most of the sandy beach at Cabarete. The hotel's Kiteboarding Center is the host of the annual Kiteboarding World Cup. ⓐ Olas de Oro, Calle Sosúa ⓣ 809 571 0680

SOSÚA

Sosúa by the Sea ££ This boutique beach resort is on the beach, yet in the heart of the town. ⓐ Calle B Phillips, Sosúa ⓣ 809 571 3222 ⓦ www.sosuabythesea.com

PUERTO PLATA & PLAYA DORADA

Occidental Allegro Playa Dorada £–££ All Inclusive resort. Offers daily activities, with plenty of watersports, three swimming pools, tennis court, a kids' club, and nightly entertainment with a casino. ⓐ Playa Dorada Complex, Puerto Plata ⓣ 809 320 3988 ⓦ www.occidentalhotels.com

SANTIAGO

Hotel Aloha Sol ££ Conveniently situated right in the city centre. ⓐ Calle del Sol 50, aptdo 1028, Santiago ⓣ 809 583 0090 ⓦ www.alohasol.com

Preparing to go

GETTING THERE

The least expensive way to get to the Dominican Republic is to book a package holiday with one of the various leading tour operators. Most companies offer deals that give the option of flight-only or combined flight and accommodation packages at very competitive prices compared to calling a resort directly. If you are flexible with your travel times and are not limited by school holidays, it is wise to take advantage of the last-minute deals offered by many of the popular websites. Weekend travel sections of your newspaper are also a likely place to find advertisements offering specials on airfare and lodging. The classified section may also prove useful in finding a private home or apartment to rent for your stay.

Many people are aware that air travel emits CO_2, which contributes to climate change. You may be interested in the possibility of lessening the environmental impact of your flight through the charity Climate Care, which offsets your CO_2 by funding environmental projects around the world. Visit ⓦ www.climatecare.org

BEFORE YOU LEAVE

The most common vaccinations recommended for those visiting are hepatitis A and typhoid, although they are not required. If you do have these inoculations, it should be at least two weeks before you leave. It is a good idea to take an anti-malaria treatment when visiting the Dominican Republic, especially if you are planning to visit places near the border with Haiti. Ask your doctor about this.

To ensure that your holiday is an enjoyable one, begin preparing well in advance to be sure everything is in order. It is a good idea to pack a small first-aid kit to carry with you, containing plasters, antiseptic cream, travel-sickness pills, insect repellent and/or bite-relief cream, antihistamine tablets, upset stomach remedies and painkillers, condoms if you plan on being sexually active (HIV is a health threat on this island), as well as sun lotion of SPF 35 or higher and after-sun cream.

If you are taking prescription medicines, ensure that you take enough for the duration of your visit as you may not be able to buy them locally.

Make sure you have sufficient travel insurance cover for your holiday, and that your policy covers you adequately for loss of possessions and valuables, for activities you might want to try – such as scuba diving, horse riding, or watersports – and for emergency medical and dental treatment, including flights home if required, especially if you suffer from any chronic health conditions.

Take sensible precautions to prevent your house from being burgled while you are away. Cancel regular deliveries so they do not pile up, indicating that you are away. Consider buying electrical timing devices that will switch lights on and off, again to give the impression that there is someone in the house. Let Neighbourhood Watch representatives know that you will be away so that they can keep a watch on your home. If you have a burglar alarm, make sure that it is serviced and working properly and is switched on when you leave (you may find that your insurance policy requires this). Ensure that a neighbour is able to gain access to the alarm to turn it off if it is set off accidentally.

ENTRY FORMALITIES

The most important documents you will need are your tickets and your passport. Check well in advance that your passport is up to date and has at least three months left to run (six months is even better). All children, including newborn babies, need their own passports now. It generally takes at least three weeks to process a passport renewal. This can be longer in the run-up to the summer months. Contact the Passport Agency for the latest information on how to renew your passport and the processing times involved. ☏ 0870 521 0410 ⓦ www.ukpa.gov.uk.

For the UK, each person (including children, even if they are travelling on their parents' passport) also requires a Tourist Card. They are available on arrival at the airport (US$10 at time of writing) or, in person or by post, in advance from the Dominican Embassy (see page 116).

You should check the details of your travel tickets well before your departure, ensuring that the timings and dates are correct.

If you are thinking of hiring a car while you are away, you will need to have your UK driving licence with you. If you want more than one driver for the car, the other drivers must have their licences too.

Because of the increasing problem of international child abduction, anyone travelling with a child who has a different surname needs to have a certified letter certifying guardianship or an original or certified copy of the child's birth certificate on their person in case there is a need to prove the relationship. For more information on this, contact the **Dominican Embassy** ⓐ 139 Inverness Terrace, Bayswater, London W2 6JF ⓣ 020 7727 6285/020 7727 3693 ⓦ www.dominicanembassy.org.uk

MONEY

The currency is the peso (RD$). US dollars are also widely accepted, especially in the high-end resorts. The currency comes in coins of 1, 5, 10 and 25 pesos or notes of 20, 50, 100, 200, 500, 1,000 and 2,000. The traditional way of carrying money, buying traveller's cheques and exchanging your currency for pesos and pesetas is becoming a thing of the past. The global economy is making the euro, pound and dollar often freely traded currencies in markets.

Banks Available to cash traveller's cheques, although the accessibility and safety of credit and debit cards has made them virtually obsolete. 'Casa de cambios' and ATMs will give equally fair exchange rates. Bank hours are usually Mon–Fri 08.00–16.00 and Sat 09.00–13.00. But if you go to a bank located in the malls the working hours extends until 19.00.

Credit cards Accepted at larger stores and hotels, and may be used at any of the ATMs found across the country. If you are depending on your credit card to make purchases, keep in mind that most retailers add a surcharge of up to 16 per cent for the service. You will most likely forfeit your right to haggle for prices, as well.

Cash machines Found nearly everywhere in populated and tourist areas, an equally secure way to receive a fair exchange rate. Some may have no access fee for cash advances; check with your bank before leaving home to learn what affiliation to use to avoid a hefty charge.

Never trust anyone who offers to exchange money on the street. Always be sure to ask for plenty of small notes (RD$100 or smaller) and some change, which is useful when trying to bargain in markets.

CLIMATE

The island's climate is generally warm – about 29°C (84°F) year-round. Waters along the Caribbean coast are temperate and perfect for swimming, and the Atlantic coast is just a bit cooler. Summer temperatures can rise up to 35°C (95°F), and can be stifling without air-conditioning. The mountain regions are far cooler, averaging a temperature of 24°C (75°F), and even below freezing at the top of Pico Duarte.

The rainy seasons here vary quite a bit by region, despite the country's small size. The Samaná Peninsula gets the most rain, with respite during the months of February and March. From May to October, expect Santo Domingo to get most of the daily downpour. The north coast has its turn come October, lasting as late as March. Fortunately, tropical rain storms come and go quickly, often cooling off a humid day instead of spoiling a holiday. The rains that can hamper a holiday are hurricanes, which typically hit the island from August through October. The eastern side of the island is usually hit the hardest, with damage ranging from flooding to complete devastation. Despite increased hurricane activity during recent years, visitors continue to come during these months. If you are near the shore when a hurricane is approaching, try to get at least several kilometres inland, and head for one of the large resorts where the facilities are well prepared.

BAGGAGE ALLOWANCES

Baggage allowances vary according to the airline, destination and the class of travel, but 20 kg (44 lb) per person is the norm for luggage that is carried in the hold. If in doubt, check your ticket – it usually tells you the weight limit. You are also allowed one item of cabin baggage weighing no more than 5 kg (11 lb) and measuring no larger than 46 by 30 by 23 cm (18 by 12 by 9 in). This restriction is more strictly enforced than it was in the past. Despite this limitation, it is a good idea to try and pack at least a day's change of clothes and anything of vital importance in your carry-on baggage in the event that the checked luggage is delayed upon arrival. Women are also allowed to carry handbags, and passengers are usually able to have their duty-free bags and coats held separately. It is a good idea to contact the airline ahead of time if you plan on bringing large or awkward items such as a pushchair, wheelchairs, golf clubs or surf board, since you may be charged extra or might not be allowed to bring them into the cabin.

Be aware of increased international security requirements, and remove any folding pocket knives or other sharp objects from carry-on baggage. When in doubt, check with your airline.

CHECK-IN, PASSPORT CONTROL & CUSTOMS

Plan to arrive at the airport a full two-and-a-half hours before your scheduled departure time for check-in. Have tickets and passport readily accessible. Find your flight number on the TV monitors located at airport entrances to find your check-in desk.

You will receive your boarding pass and your luggage will be checked. It is very important that you keep your luggage receipts – you will not be allowed to leave the airport in the Dominican Republic with your luggage without these as proof of ownership.

Find your designated departure gate. Boarding will begin about thirty minutes before flight time. Those travelling with small children or the elderly should listen for the first boarding call, which gives these groups special preference.

During your stay

AIRPORTS

The main airports are:

International Las Américas, Santo Domingo ℹ 809 947 2225
International Gregorio Luperón, Puerto Plata ℹ 809 291 0000
International Arroyo Barril, Samaná ℹ 809 248 2566
International María Montéz, Barahona ℹ 809 524 4144
International La Romana ℹ 809 813 9000
International Punta Cana ℹ 809 959 2376

Arrival

Tourist Cards Every visitor who comes to the Dominican Republic must first purchase a Tourist Card, which enables the holder to legally stay in the country for 90 days. You will need to get this card before passing through immigration and customs, and it is important that you do not lose it since it is needed in order to leave the country as well. If you lose your card, you will have to pay a fine and buy another one. No matter what country you are flying in from or where you hold your passport, the Tourist Card (at the time of writing) must be paid for with $10 in US currency; keep in mind that upon departure there will be an exit tax of US$20. If you want to stay longer than 90 days, you are required to get an extension. There is an office on the Malecón in Santo Domingo at Centro de Los Héroes (ℹ 809 534 8060) that processes requests quickly. Fines for overstays can be as high as RD$5,000.

Embarkation/disembarkation cards You will have filled these out during your flight or passage and will need to have them ready to present to immigration officers, along with your Tourist Card and other documentation.

Immigration & customs When approaching immigration, have your passport, Tourist Card and embarkation/disembarkation card ready. After you collect your luggage, it needs to be checked through customs.

Export restrictions & limits Be sure to check with your own country's import restrictions and limits as well, especially if you are planning on

bringing home a large number of cigars or a quantity of alcohol.
The following are restricted:

- anything over 100 years old without an Official Export Certificate
- mahogany products
- tortoiseshell
- unpolished amber (raw amber).

COMMUNICATIONS

Telephones

If you need to call from a payphone, it is easier to purchase a
Communicard, available in stores nearly everywhere. Dial 611 for instructions
in English, and dial 1411 for directory information. You may also wish to
check with your mobile phone provider about global roaming options,
since there is adequate mobile phone service in the country. If you have a
mobile phone that is not in use or would like to buy one there, prepaid
cards may be purchased and activated once you arrive.

Internet access

The growing popularity and demand for Internet access has resulted in
several options for the traveller looking to get connected:

In-room service Top hotels and resorts now offer free Internet access,
while others may charge per minute or hour.

TELEPHONING THE DOMINICAN REPUBLIC

To telephone the Dominican Republic from the UK, first dial
00 1 then the national area code (809) followed by the seven-digit
number.
To make calls within the Dominican Republic, you must dial 1 809
for Santo Domingo, or 1 829 for other cities and mobile phones.

CALLING ABROAD

To call abroad dial 011 followed by your country code (UK +44) and
the phone number.

All-inclusive resort Internet cafés The most expensive, but the least susceptible to blackouts, thanks to generator backup. Surf the net, burn CDs, print or send digital photos, all without leaving beachside.
Internet cafés Rates are by the hour and quite inexpensive; services vary but usually include broadband connection and webcams.

Post

If you want your postcards to arrive home before you do, and within a month, you will have to post them special delivery – and even that does not guarantee anything.

ELECTRICITY

The Dominican Republic uses the 110 to 125 volts AC, 60 Hz, flat-pronged plugs electrical system (the same as is used in Canada and the USA), so you will need to bring a travel adapter plub. These are readily available in the UK at electrical shops or major chemists. Power cuts are a very common occurrence, and it is a good idea to pack at least one flashlight with fresh batteries. Large hotels and many shops have backup generators.

EMERGENCIES

In case of emergency dial 911
Police, Santo Domingo ☎ 809 682 2151 Ⓦ www.policianacional.gov.do
Politur (Tourist Police) ☎ 809 222 2036
Ambulance (Movimed) ☎ 809 535 1080

British Embassy ⓐ Avenida 27 de Febrero 233, Edificio Corominas Pepín, 7th Floor, Santo Domingo ☎ 809 472 7111
Ⓦ www.britishembassy.gov.uk
British Honorary Consul ⓐ Calle Beller 51, Puerto Plata ☎ 809 586 4244

GETTING AROUND

Car hire & driving Major international car rental companies and several locally owned outfits have offices located directly at each major airport. A valid driver's licence from your country of origin is sufficient to be allowed to operate a vehicle here. If you do hire a car, it is a good idea to always keep your petrol tank at least half full – petrol stations close very early and often run out of fuel (purchase it when you can). Become acquainted with your spare tyre (and be sure your car is supplied with this and a car-jack) – punctured tyres are common. When driving through a large puddle after rainstorms, do not take your foot off the accelerator entirely. Keep enough exhaust flowing out of the exhaust-pipe to prevent water from entering, to avoid stalling. Do not simply trust a road map: ask your hotel or host for help with directions and then a local whom you can understand well – often maps are misleading and will bring you onto trails, not roads.

Motoconchos These various two-wheeled vehicles, offered for hire, are an extremely cheap but equally dangerous way to get around; multitudes of tourists are injured and killed riding on them each year.

Buses These are an efficient and inexpensive way to get around. You can choose between the *primera* bus with air conditioning and toilets to take you on longer trips, or a *gua-gua* for short trips around town to save on taxi fares, depending on your destination and needs. The latter is slow and usually crowded, since it makes many stops and is the main method of transportation for locals. Larger cities offer one step up from that, with limited stops and air conditioning. Bus schedules can be found at all major tourist offices. Even first-class bus rides are inexpensive.

Taxis Cabs usually wait at hotels or other taxi parks such as the airport. If you are in need of a taxi or anticipate needing one, have the phone number handy to call the service. Always ask the price ahead of time and have the exact change ready.

HEALTH

Your exposure to any potential infectious disease will depend greatly on your activities during your stay. Those who plan to stay within the perimeters of an all-inclusive resort will likely not need to take as many precautions as travellers bound for a week-long hike up Pico Duarte, but one's own physical condition should also be taken into consideration. Discuss the issue thoroughly with your doctor if there are any concerns.

Water in the Dominican Republic should not be swallowed, even to brush your teeth. Unless you are staying at a very high-end resort hotel, use bottled water for anything that touches your mouth. This is especially true for those who are elderly or ill or otherwise susceptible to infection. It is very important, however, to drink plenty of fluids, including water, during your stay, especially when the temperatures are high, since dehydration can be a problem. The hot climate, change in diet, and often increased alcohol consumption that accompany many holidays encourage this condition, and it is wise to head it off early with several bottles of water each day to prevent symptoms such as dizziness, headaches, muscle cramps, and dark urine.

If you need a doctor during your visit, try one of the following.

Santo Domingo:
Cedimat Ⓐ Calle Ortega y Gasset, Plaza de la Salud ① 809 565 9989
Ⓦ www.cedimat.com
Clínica Abel Ⓐ González Ave. Abraham Lincoln 953 ① 809 227 2235
Clinica Abreu Ⓐ Calle Beller 42 esq. Ave Independencia ① 809 688 4411

Other cities:
Centro Medico Bournigal Ⓐ A Mota, Puerto Plata ① 809 586 2342
Centro Medico Central Ⓐ Romana, La Romana ① 809 532 3333
Centro Medico Punta Cana Ⓐ Carretera Friusa ① 809 552 1506
Clínica Corominas Ⓐ Calle Restauración 57, Santiago ① 809 580 1171
Clínica Santo Tomás Ⓐ Calle J. Mota 47, Barahona ① 809 524 2349
Hospiten Bávaro Ⓐ Carretera Bávaro ① 809 686 1414

LANGUAGE
Dominicans do their best to cater to the needs of English-speaking visitors, but it is considered polite, and sometimes necessary, to know a few simple phrases in Spanish to show respect and make your travels easier.

OPENING HOURS

Shops and boutiques typically open at 08.30 and close for siesta between noon and 14.00, reopening until 18.30. In heavily populated and tourist areas, you may find extended store hours and perhaps even stores open during siesta to meet tourist demands. Most restaurants in any resort region open by 10.00 and will not close until at least 22.00, most likely later, and are open daily, unless family operated.

TIME DIFFERENCE

The Dominican Republic maintains Eastern Standard Time, which is five hours behind GMT.

TIPPING

As a result of terribly low wages, tipping is very important to those employed in the service and tourism industry. In some jobs, as in other countries, it is expected that tips will be received and therefore little or no salary is paid. As long as service was acceptable, it is customary to tip waiters, porters, housekeepers and tour guides:

- Leaving 10 to 15 per cent of the total restaurant bill is average for waiters.
- Leave your tips in cash when paying by credit card to ensure your server receives it.
- Consider using US dollars – one dollar will be more appreciated than its equivalent in pesos.
- Housekeepers receive about US$1–2 per night; it is best to leave this in an envelope marked 'gracias' on the bureau each morning.

TRAVELLERS WITH DISABILITIES

With so many choices of brand-new, all-inclusive resorts designed for tourists with every type of need, visitors with disabilities should have a much easier time getting the most out of their stay than just a decade or two ago. Most public facilities and museums in the country are not set up for wheelchairs

FIND THE LATEST HOTSPOT

Get more from your holiday and discover the best restaurants, bars, beaches and family-friendly attractions with these handy pocket guides. Our wide range covers over 45 destinations:

Algarve
Bali
Brazil
Bulgaria:
  Black Sea Resorts
Corfu
Corsica
Costa Blanca
Costa Brava &
Costa Dorada
Costa del Sol &
Costa de Almeria
Côte D'Azur
Crete
Croatia
Cuba
Cyprus
Dominican Republic
Egypt:
  Red Sea Resorts
Fuerteventura
Gibraltar
Goa
Gran Canaria
Guernsey
Halkidiki
Hawaii
Ibiza
Ionian Islands

Jamaica
Jersey
Kenya:
  Indian Ocean
  Resorts
Lanzarote
Madeira
Maldives
Mallorca
Malta
Menorca
Mexico
Morocco
Neapolitan Riviera
Orlando
Rhodes & Kos
Santorini
Sardinia
Sicily
Sri Lanka
Tenerife
Thailand
Tunisia
Turkey –
  Aegean Coast
  Lycian Coast
  Mediterranean
  Coast

Available from all good bookshops, your local Thomas Cook travel store or browse and buy on-line at www.thomascookpublishing.com

Thomas Cook
Publishing

ACKNOWLEDGEMENTS

We would like to thank all the photographers, pictures libraries and organisations for the loan of the photographs reproduced in this book, to whom copyright in the photograph belongs: Alamy pages 26, 42; Corbis page 70, 79, 81, 83,109; Dreamstime/R Lerich page 52; Getty Images page 29; Pictures Colour Library pages 68, 73, 88; Tips page 10–11, 15, 33, 36, 44, 65, 93, 111; Thomas Cook pages 1, 5, 13, 50, 61, 62, 95, 98, 103, 105, 107; World Pictures/Photoshot pages 25, 31, 47, 57, 75.

Project editors: Catherine Burch & Robert Wilkinson
Proofreader: Claire Boobbyer
Indexer: Marie Lorimer

Send your thoughts to
books@thomascook.com

- Found a beach bar, peaceful stretch of sand or must-see sight that we don't feature?

- Like to tip us off about any information that needs a little updating?

- Want to tell us what you love about this handy little guidebook and more importantly how we can make it even handier?

Then here's your chance to tell all! Send us ideas, discoveries and recommendations today and then look out for your valuable input in the next edition of this title.

Email to the above address or write to:
HotSpots Series Editor, Thomas Cook Publishing, PO Box 227, Coningsby Road, Peterborough PE3 8SB, UK.